I Will Enter His Gates

A Walk With God

JAN REA JOHNSON

I Will Enter His Gates
A Walk With God
All Rights Reserved.
Copyright © 2019 Jan Rea Johnson
v2.0

The opinions expressed in this manuscript are solely the opinions of the author and do not represent the opinions or thoughts of the publisher. The author has represented and warranted full ownership and/or legal right to publish all the materials in this book.

This book may not be reproduced, transmitted, or stored in whole or in part by any means, including graphic, electronic, or mechanical without the express written consent of the publisher except in the case of brief quotations embodied in critical articles and reviews.

Outskirts Press, Inc.
http://www.outskirtspress.com

ISBN: 978-1-9772-0747-0

Library of Congress Control Number: 2019901401

Cover Photo © 2019 www.gettyimages.com. All rights reserved - used with permission.

Outskirts Press and the "OP" logo are trademarks belonging to Outskirts Press, Inc.

PRINTED IN THE UNITED STATES OF AMERICA

In memory of Robert Howard Rea III
December 21, 1946- May 2, 1985
For my children
Especially Nick, Sara and Kyle

AUTHOR'S NOTE

After my husband, Howard Rea died in 1985, I started going through his desk. I had known that he was constantly writing in his journal, but what I found there within the pages of that book were thoughts so rich, that I knew they had to be made available to others to read and gain inspiration.

Going through any traumatic experience is difficult. I found myself seeking any books or information, or people to talk to who were either going through the same thing or had made it through to the other side of trials and tribulations.

I didn't think it would make sense to just write the notes from his journal, and so decided to write a memoir. All conversations are the essence of truth in the situation. Some names and places have been changed. All Bible references are from the New American Standard Bible.

My hope is that this gives strength to the weary, hope for the moment and salvation to those who seek it.

Table of Contents

Prologue: Warrenton, Oregon 1985 I
Chapter 1: Warrenton 1982 1
Chapter 2: Warrenton 1983 12
Chapter 3: 1975 16
Chapter 4: Tuba City, Arizona 1976 22
Chapter 5: Hammond, Oregon 1978 28
Chapter 6: Warrenton 32
Chapter 7: Warrenton 36
Chapter 8 40
Chapter 9: Warrenton 44
Chapter 10 50
Chapter 11 51
Chapter 12: Warrenton 55
Chapter 13: Portland, Oregon 57
Chapter 14: Portland 70
Chapter 15: Portland 80
Chapter 16: Warrenton 83
Chapter 17: Warrenton 91
Chapter 18 113
Chapter 19: Portland 116
Chapter 20: Astoria, Oregon 122
Chapter 21: Warrenton 130
Chapter 22 134
Chapter 23: Warrenton 149
Chapter 24 155
Chapter 25 162

Chapter 26: Warrenton 168
Chapter 27: Seattle, Washington 174
Chapter 28 182
Chapter 29: Warrenton 185
Chapter 30: Warrenton 188
Chapter 31: Warrenton 191
Epilogue: Five Months After 196
Book Club Questions 225
Acknowledgments 228
About The Author 229

PROLOGUE

1985
Warrenton, Oregon

RED AND AMBER lights whir rhythmically, reflecting on the bedroom mirror. I am only aware of the pulse of my heart as it beats rapidly in my ears.

"The ambulance is here, Mom," Nick says. "Mom? The ambulance is here." He tugs on my arm. I look through the window, and then at my son. I still can't believe this was happening. I knew it was only going to be one more year. That's the answer I had gotten last April when I had asked God how much longer all this was going to last. But still, Howard Rea, my husband, had been doing so well. Even tonight he had said,

"Well, I guess the doctors are going to be wrong again. They said two years and look how well I'm doing!"

Just tonight, I had gone to my friend Marianne Reed's to spend a respite evening visiting. Howard had taken care of the kids tonight alone. Granted, Sara was six and able to do a lot of things for herself and I'm sure Nick helped get three-year-old Kyle into his pj's. Nevertheless, Howard had read them stories, gotten them tucked in and managed mostly on his own.

"How did everything go?" I asked when I had returned. "I didn't get any frantic phone calls from you!"

"No, it was great. I'm glad you were able to get a break."

I give him a goodnight peck on his bearded cheek and headed to bed. "I'll see you about 11:00. I still want to do some Bible reading and write some more in my journal," he says.

"I won't see you," I reply, as usual, not realizing this would be our last conversation. "I'll be sleeping. Goodnight." I purse my lips and smack a kiss towards him.

It's 3:00 AM now. Howard comes into the bedroom calling my name, Jaahhn. Slurred. Anxious. I bolt up in bed, awakening from a deep sleep.

"What's going on? Are you having a seizure?" He's holding his head with both of his hands.

"My head. My head hurts. It hurts!" he moans.

I grab him by the shoulders and sit him down on the bed. What should I do? What should I do? His eyes are vacant. He falls back onto the handmade quilt of our king-sized bed. I look around, like there might be an answer on the wall, or the ceiling. Like everything else on this long road, there might magically appear writing on the wall to guide me. Was this it? Was this how he was going to die? He didn't want to die in a hospital. But what should I do? I grab his bottle of phenobarbital from the nightstand. My shaky hands open the bottle and take one out. I grab the bottle of water next to the bed and try to get him to swallow. He begins to spasm and wretch. I look around for something- a towel, a bowl, anything. I run upstairs to get Nick. He's only eleven, but he has been my little man, there when I needed him. And right now, I need him to stay with his dad while I make frantic phone calls. Who should I call? It's 3:00 in the morning. I try our friend Nancy who's a nurse from church and has been with us on more than one occasion.

Ring.

I listen for Howard.

Ring.

Hurry and pick up.

Ring.

After the fourth ring I hang up. Any person in their right mind would be sleeping right now. Now what? God, what should I do? I could try Marianne, but she'll tell me to call an ambulance. Ok then, that's what it's going to be. I'm sorry Howard. I know you don't want to go this way. I know how much you hate hospitals.

I open the front door and let the men in. They wheel in a gurney, through the kitchen, down the hall, around the corner into our bedroom. Now Howard lays on the bed, eyes closed, his paralyzed right-hand twitching. They lift him onto the gurney, cover him with a warm blanket and roll him to the ambulance, this made easier because of the newly installed ramp.

I stand, stunned, staring at the empty place in the bed. The place that will no longer hold my husband. Lord, is this it? Is this the end? And then, an audible voice.

"Yea, though I walk through the valley of the shadow of death, I will fear no evil." I look around to see which one of the men had said it. No, they were outside putting him into the ambulance.

"Yea, though I walk through the valley of the shadow of death, I will fear no evil," I whisper. "This is it, Lord, isn't it? He's going home, isn't he? He's going home!"

CHAPTER 1

1982
Warrenton

"HELP ME LIFT this box, Mare. I can't get it by myself." Marianne walks into the kitchen to help me with the other end of a box of toys.

"Where do they go?" she asks as she heaves up her end.

"Upstairs," I say. "We'll put them in the center room between the two bedrooms. That will be the kids' play room." I carefully back my way down the hall, through the study and towards the wooden stairs. I can't believe we are actually moving into a house with some land. And a four-bedroom house at that! We'd gotten it for a song. We were able to buy it on a contract and money down that we had made from selling our HOA house. We had purchased that house new two years earlier for $20,000 and had made a tidy $20,000 profit. Now our payments were only going to be $135 a month, a price we could afford.

Howard, Nick and I had moved to Astoria, Oregon two years earlier. It had been more of an adventure than a thought-out plan. We had been teaching in Tuba City, Arizona on the Navajo Reservation. Situated in northern Arizona, it was high desert. There were magnificent red streaked hills and mesas. Occasionally you would see an oasis, green trees and grass in an isolated spot, surrounded by several hogans, round, mud houses. We would go out to eat on Friday nights at the only restaurant in town. We filled ourselves on Navajo Tacos which were made with fry bread, beans, lettuce and tomato. On weekends, we'd go to the Trading Post to buy groceries. There wasn't a huge selection, but it was sufficient. The Trading Post also carried hand spun, hand dyed yarn which hung from the rafters. Eye candy for someone like me who loves to knit. There was jewelry made by local artists. Earrings and necklaces of silver and turquoise. On the shelves stood Kachina Dolls carved from wood, painted to look like their respective god, and clothed in costume. Walls were lined with hand woven rugs of handspun wool. Some depicted people and towns. Some had jagged lines. There was Anasazi pottery, delicately painted, black and white. Handmade baskets were stacked on shelves, each with their unique design representing different aspects of their faith. It was definitely a culture rich in the arts. But Tuba City was so small. So isolated. I wasn't sure that I wanted my three-year-old son to grow up there.

"Golly, you couldn't have put in a few more books or something to make this box heavier could you?" Marianne asks as she strains to hold up her end. I back up the stairs slowly.

"Wimp," I reply. She sticks her tongue out at me. We heave the box up onto the landing. "You've got to quit going to so many garage sales! Which room is which?" Marianne asks, exhaling deeply.

"The one over the carport is Nick's, the other will be Sara's. I'm going to keep baby Kyle downstairs next to our room." We walk into Nick's new room and look out the single pane aluminum window. Fir trees dot the distant hills, their silhouettes black against the pale blue sky. A herd of beef cattle roam the thirty acres ahead. An old farmhouse sits on the neighboring property showing years of strain on the siding and falling gutters. A golden lab runs along a cedar fence, jumping over fallen fence posts. A Spruce tree in the midst of our field could have been perfect for Jack to climb to the giant's castle. Hundreds of Starlings chatter noisily in the huge branches proclaiming their claim on the territory. An old railroad track stands between the large back yard and the back field. How many freight cars or people had passed by here taking fish to markets beyond, or logs hewn in the woods, or perhaps those headed to California looking for gold. Now there were only overgrown blackberry bushes covering the yard. A rusty old bedspring is sticking up from the midst of the earth. The sun reflects on old broken beer bottles with their necks protruding from the soil which peek out between weeds and bunch grass. Barbed wire loops in and out of the mound, reminding me of my first attempts at cursive in second grade.

"You've got your work cut out for you, girl," Marianne says, shaking her head.

"Yeah, there is a lot to do." I look at the cheap plywood paneling, the peeling wallpaper, the ripped linoleum. It took four washings with ammonia water to get the smoke grime off of the windows.

"That's probably why we could afford it! We'll have to tear out all those blackberry bushes, paint the outside, and take a load or two to the dump."

"A load or two... that's an understatement! But it does have good bones," she says as we start for the stairs.

"The stairs could use carpeting and a railing to begin with," I say, thinking of nine-month-old Kyle. He'll be learning to walk before you know it.

"All in good time," she says. "Look at how long it's taken to get our house fixed up. Golly, at least we don't have bats flying around in the attic anymore!"

I laugh. "Yeah, haven't seen any bats around here. Yet." I say.

"You never know," she says, glancing at the attic door. We head to the living room with the goal of decreasing the mountains of boxes.

The first time I saw Marianne was a year after I had opened the preschool in 1976.

"Do you have room for two more two-year olds?" she asked. "I've just started a job and I'm new to the area. This is McKenzie." She held up a small hand to me. "And this is Scott," she said as she nodded her chin into his straight black hair and adjusted him on her hip. His jet-black squinty eyes twinkled as he grinned at us. A bit of drool ran down his mouth and onto the scarf tied around his neck.

"I know McKenzie will be fine- it's Scott I'm concerned about. He has Cerebral Palsy. Is anyone here knowledgeable about CP?"

"No," I said. "But we're open to new adventures! Hi Scott, hi McKenzie! It's nice to meet you. There are all kinds of toys and lots of kids to play with here." Scott gives a crooked smile and raises his atrophied hand slightly in a wave.

I had always thought of myself as being accepting of all people regardless of their nationalities and physical abilities-- or not. And I loved a challenge. So of course, I said we'd be delighted to take them.

"Although he's three, Scott still needs to be strapped into a high chair. Cut his food up small so that he doesn't choke. He'll be having surgery soon on his salivary glands, so he won't drool so much."

Marianne showed us some American Sign Language we could use to communicate with him. And actually, it wasn't for him to understand us, for he could hear perfectly well. He just didn't have the ability to speak, and the sign language was in order to teach him to communicate with us.

Marianne puts Scott down. I take him by the hand and lead him and McKenzie to the play area. I introduce them to Andrew and Amy who are romping in the playhouse.

"When is your baby due?" Marianne asks me, eyeing my huge belly.

"Not till January. I still have three months!"

"No way! You're way too big! You're sure it's not twins?" she says.

"Nope, I just get big!" I grin and rub my belly.

Marianne and I tromp back downstairs for more boxes. Through the north window I can see Sara and Nick playing in the woods It is cozy and there are enormous cedar trees towering over them. Sara spreads her arms to keep her balance as she walks carefully along a huge branch that curves into a bench low to the ground. McKenzie runs over and grabs her hand to make sure she won't fall. Sara's cropped blonde hair is blown back by the gentle breeze. Her green coveralls house the flowered button-down shirt I had just made for her. I smile. She is another of God's blessings.

The year we married in 1976, Howard and I decided to try for a baby. I got pregnant right away. We were so excited the first time we heard the swish swish swish of the heartbeat. LIFE Magazine had come out with a book that showed pictures of week by week fetal development. Nick, Howard and I sat cozily on the couch and examined each photograph. Imagine, she (it would be a girl, right?) at six weeks already has hands and feet. Her heart was beating. She even has eyelids. The book said that synapses were forming in her brain. Maybe she was thinking about her new home. Maybe she's thinking about her new big brother. How could they take such amazing pictures? Ultra-sound wasn't even in the vocabulary yet. Scientists were able to invent a machine to show the miracle of life.

Four months later, after I'd started feeling baby Alicia kick, after I'd picked out a name, after I'd started buying clothes at garage sales, I began to bleed. The spotting went on for a week.

"Don't worry," said my friends. "A lot of women bleed when they're preggers." But I was no longer feeling any fluttering and my breasts were no longer tender.

Several weeks later, we had driven out to Denver to visit my mother, who had a new professorship as an Art Education Instructor at Denver University.

"Jan, maybe you should see my doctor. It isn't right that you should be bleeding. I'm wondering if you've miscarried. Have you passed anything large enough to be a fetus?" she asked me. I lowered my head. Tears began to well up. I whispered, "No".

She made an appointment.

"Well dear," the doctor said as he put a hand on my shoulder, "You've miscarried." I was confused. How could that be? I was still showing.

"But I haven't lost anything. Shouldn't there be something more than just blood?" I asked. My stomach lurched.

He shrugged. "Your urine test shows negative."

He wrote out a prescription and sent me home. The following week, after I had returned to our home in Warrenton, while going to the bathroom my uterus gave way. In the toilet was a round, red blob, the size of my fist. I had always thought that when it happened, I would cut it open to see my baby. But I couldn't. I just couldn't bring myself to reach in and touch and hold it. I just flushed the toilet and watched as it swirled away.

"Goodbye, sweetheart." I turned and wept as my husband held me close.

Two months later, I was pregnant again. This time, I was three months into it when I began to bleed. Again. My heart dropped to my stomach. I couldn't believe that God would allow this to happen to me twice. What was wrong with me that I couldn't carry a child? Why couldn't this have happened when I was single and pregnant? Not that I didn't love Nick. But wouldn't that have made a lot more sense? He was the result of a two-month fling. Here I was married now, and ready to have a little family. But God seemed to have other plans. I couldn't understand it. And it didn't make the prospect any more forgiving.

I developed a massive headache. I tried to rest. No relief. I picked up Chronicles of Narnia and only got through a few pages. Unbearable, consuming throbbing.

Maybe a shower will help. I let the hot water pour down on me, hoping it would alleviate the pain. I didn't want to take any aspirin, because I might hurt the baby. I rubbed my hands over my swollen belly.

Howard convinced me to go to the doctor. As we drove the eight miles to Seaside, I laid my head on the window, not seeing the rain.

Not hearing the windshield wipers swishing back and forth. Thoughts of what was to come and what had been, consumed me. What if it's already dead? Will I pass this one the same way? Will I have the courage this time to hold it, this precious little life?

The doctor immediately put me into the hospital. After I slipped into a god-awful pale green hospital gown, I held my arm out as the nurse poked and prodded, trying to find my vein for the IV. Isn't this bad enough without you having to be inefficient? I was wheeled into a surgical room. The blue walls seemed to close in on me. Instruments clinked onto the metal tray.

"Legs in the stirrups, spread your legs. Relax," the doctor said. Relax? Relax?? What is he thinking! What is he doing? What is he going to do?

Probing, he said, "Ok, I'm removing part of a leg now." A leg? He's got my baby. I'll be able to see it this time. Maybe hold it.

And, "I've got a hand." I could feel my eyes tear up. What is he doing? He's tearing up my baby! I wanted to jump up and knock his hands away. I wanted to claw his eyes out. How could the nurses watch this? How could he describe it in detail? Doesn't he know I'm here listening? Is there no compassion?

That night, I cried softly in the hospital bed. So quiet. So lonely. God surely didn't want me to have a baby. I was to go through life with just Nick and not be able to give Howard the joy of our union. Howard treated Nick as if he was his own, but I wanted to be able to give him his own child. Surely that was a gift that I could give him.

Rain beat upon the window. I watched the water trickle down the pane. The doctor came in and stood next to my bed.

"It's not all that bad, young lady. Many women miscarry. Give it six months and try again." Six months is an eternity. What does he know about what's bad and what's not?

I marked the calendar. Six months, to the day, we held off. Then we began trying again. I missed my next period and got a pregnancy test from the drug store. My adrenaline ran as I unwrapped the package with shaky hands. Did I even want to know? I could just wait a few more months and see. I held the little plastic cup between my legs trying to keep all the stream into the container and miss my hand I set the cup on the counter, reread the directions and placed the test paper into the urine. I set the timer on the stove for the required three minutes. How can a mere three minutes last so long? I was pacing, looking out the window three times, peeking on Nick playing Legos in his room, looking at the clock, picking up a magazine, putting it down. I jumped as the timer went off. I took slow steps down the hall. What if it's just a late period? What if I am pregnant again and am going to just lose this one too. I walked into the bathroom, like in a dream, surrounded by the surreal and walking in slow motion. I pulled out the tab and it was a yes! I ran in to Howard and showed him the results. He eyed me skeptically. Anxiety forced it's way in. I thought he would be excited. He put his hands on my shoulders and looked into my eyes. "I hope this one's a keeper," he said. I gave an imperceptible nod.

    I marked off the calendar at six weeks and went into my first doctor's visit. He said I was pregnant. Duh! I knew that. My breasts were tender. I would nod off while stirring the pot for dinner. The doctor said that everything seemed to be fine. Tears welled up. I let out a deep breath not realizing how I had been holding it in and drove home.

    When, at four months, I felt the little feet kicking my insides, I became anxious. This was when I had lost the first baby. I didn't want to place a name on the baby. There's a good chance that this one won't make it either, I thought. I had told no one that I was pregnant. It would make it too real. What if I lost this one too? I didn't want people looking at me thinking the inevitable was to happen again. I didn't want that gulf that happens when people grieve for you and don't know how to make it better.

    I passed up the baby clothes and strollers at garage sales. I still had the baby clothes my mother had saved for me from when my brother and sisters and I were little. I could use them to begin with.

At seven months, I was large. No, not large, huge. Enormous. Some people give birth when they look as big as I was. Clerks in the store would ask if I were pregnant with twins.

I would lay on my back in bed and Howard and I would watch my stomach sway from one side to the other. Nick would crawl into bed with us and giggle as the baby would move from one side of my stomach to the other.

"Nick, grab on right here." I put his small hand on the baby's sharp heel that protruded from my belly. He tried to grab it. It would move. He would giggle. He would try to grab onto the little foot again. He giggled again.

Advertisements reminded us that it was only four weeks till Christmas. The winter rains had started, and the skies were constantly grey. The baby was due in January. Jeannie had asked me to go Christmas shopping in Portland with her. She had left her twin boys with her mother and we had a day to ourselves. Early that morning I had felt the first pull at my lower back, signaling the first contractions. I ignored them, thinking they were Braxton hicks. I had had false pains for some time now. I was sure this was nothing different.

We went to the mall, purchasing gifts here and there. While standing in Macy's, I looked at the racks, pretending I was looking at the clothes. Here comes another one. I put my hands onto my stomach as the muscles tightened. This one was stronger. What should I do? I didn't want Jeannie to be worried. And I wasn't sure this was really it, but the pains were getting stronger. Should I call Howard?

The plan was that we would have this baby at home. Our friend Shary would watch Nick while Elizabeth, a local midwife, would come to the house. I had met with her and she seemed competent. After all, I had delivered my friend's baby in a log cabin, having never witnessed a birth before. And all the women in the Bible had their babies at home. Why couldn't I? There were far more healthy babies, than not. When I had Nick, it was in Phoenix, Arizona in an enormous hospital. Room after room lined a long corridor. It was like a baby factory. I could hear the woman in the room next to me screaming. With this baby, I couldn't fathom the thought of another enema and frightening, impersonal hospital staff.

I gripped the pole next to the wool winter coats, price tags hung from their sleeves. Jeannie looked over at me. I smiled weakly and held my belly till the tightness subsided. I still didn't want her to know; she would worry, and I didn't think this was the real thing. This baby wasn't due until January.

"Are you ok?" she asked. I nodded weakly.

"You don't look ok," she said. We finished our shopping and headed out to the car. I stopped briefly along the way while another pain, stronger this time and closer than the others, took hold. I clasped my enormous belly and felt the constriction of the muscles. When they relaxed, I maneuvered my way into the car.

"Jeannie, I think I'm going to have this baby," I said. She looked over at me, hands still on the keys at the ignition.

"Why didn't you tell me?" she said. Her eyes large, a little annoyed, anxious. "I knew it!"

"I didn't think this was really it," I said. She buckled her seat belt and said, "Well, let's get going then."

She drove the hour and a half to Seaside as fast as she could without breaking the law. Really, where were the cops when you needed them?

We found the nearest pay phone at the Dairy Queen near Banks to call Howard. My mind was racing. What should I do? Should I go home? I wasn't ready. I hadn't done the nesting thing yet. The clothes and crib were still in the garage and hadn't been washed. I dug into my purse and found a quarter. I inserted it into the phone.

"This call requires seventy-five cents," the operator said. I inserted another two quarters. It was ringing!

"Howard, we're going to have a baby!" I said.

"Now?" he asked.

"Yes, now!" I said. "And I don't know what to do."

"Just meet me at Providence Hospital in Seaside. I'll take Nick to

Shary's and then meet you there," Howard said.

Jeannie and I arrived at 9:20 p.m. The doctor and Howard were there waiting. The nurse prepped me and a half hour later, I had an eight-pound baby girl. Healthy and pink and cute as a bug's ear. I took a shower and then wrapped her up and we headed to the car. I wasn't going to stay overnight in a hospital that I hadn't even planned to have a baby in in the first place. It never occurred to me that I might have had her in the car. God's grace is sufficient.

"Uh oh," Howard said as he looked in the rear-view mirror. Red lights were flashing. He pulled the Subaru over to the side of the road. I held baby Sara Eliza tightly in my arms. Like Sarah and Elizabeth of the Bible, we'd waited so long for her.

"Let me see your driver's license please," the officer said leaning towards Howard's open window.

Howard pulled out his license.

"I'm wondering why the car was weaving," he said as he looked inside and saw me with my new bundle in my arms.

"My wife and I just had a baby," he told the officer. The man shone his flashlight onto me and the precious little one.

"Go ahead then," he said, "I'll escort you home."

We stumbled into the house, weary, but oh, so full of joy, laid our beautiful one in bed with us and fell sound asleep.

Sara runs over to watch her big brother Nick who has his collection of GI Joes strategically placed among little stick forts with leaf paths. I watch as he manipulates them into the right position. I can see his mouth move slightly as he talks for them. If I speak to him now, he would never hear me. He is in a completely different world.

The sun sparkles through the branches of the apple tree. White blossoms blanket them. A swallowtail butterfly flits through the branches. It could be a picture in a travel magazine, but it isn't. It is our new home.

CHAPTER **2**

1983
Warrenton

HOWARD ROLLS OVER in bed and drapes his arm around me.

"Are we still planning to work on the bathroom?" he mumbles.

"Mhmm," I reply, not wanting to get up yet. Not sure what a day ahead of blazing new territory will look like.

What did we know about remodeling? Not much. But we had a vague idea. A very vague idea. And Rudy Krueger, Howard's best friend said he'd help us. Wasn't he a carpenter? Or at least he'd know how to hold a hammer? That was more than Howard or I had had experience with.

"Hand me that crow bar, Jan," Howard said. I pass it to him. "I think I'm going to quit teaching." *Skriek*. He pulls out a nail.

"What will you do instead?" I ask. There goes our steady income. And insurance. I roll my eyes. Would it be too much to ask for him to stick with something secure?

"I don't know, but I hate teaching sixth grade with white kids. They are so incredibly rude." *Skriek*. "It's not like on the reservation. Those kids were so polite, and they wanted to learn. You could have fun with them. Here it's more like work and I hate it. The kids are so rude." *Skriek.* He takes the 2x4 from the wall and lays it on the floor in the hall.

My thoughts wander back to when I first met him. I had just graduated from Arizona State University and was living in a rented house in a quiet Scottsdale neighborhood. My neighbor, Sheila, had told me about a job in Tuba City, which was five hours north of Phoenix. Well, technically six if you went the speed limit. Sheila had a friend who was the principal there. I could see adventure around the corner, so I applied for a first-grade position. She drove me there for an interview and I was accepted on the spot. I didn't realize at the time that they were so desperate for teachers they would accept just about anyone.

The double-wide trailer that was provided for teachers had a charm of its own. My little home had two bedrooms- one for me and one for year two-year-old Nick. Each evening I listened as someone poured his heart and soul into his drums. The sound reverberated off the tin of the neighboring trailers. Who it could be?

It was a balmy evening when I looked out the window and saw him. His tall, lean figure was silhouetted against the sunset as he shut the door of his neighboring trailer and locked it, then climbed into his yellow jeep. I found myself going to the window often just to see if I could sneak a peek at him. I also noted that he was the only one I saw heading to church on Sunday mornings.

It was a beautiful September evening. The air was beginning to get a little crisp in the mornings and evenings, unlike Scottsdale, which was always hot. Nick and I were in the yard playing ball when he came over and introduced himself.

"Hey," Howard said and leaned on the fence. I looked up and smiled. My stomach butterflied. I didn't really know anyone here except Claudia, the second-grade teacher who lived next door. And although I enjoyed her company, I would far more enjoy the company of a man.

"My name's Howard." He held out his hand. It was warm and

strong. "You're new here. How do you like teaching here so far?"

"It's going pretty well. I've got a huge class! Forty-one first graders in one room can be overwhelming for a new teacher. What do you teach?" Brilliant blue eyes. Long eyelashes.

"I'm a sixth-grade teacher. I love my kids. They are really polite, and we have a lot of fun together. Where are you from?" he asked.

"Scottsdale."

"Long ways!"

"Five-hour drive," I said. "I won't be going *there* every weekend! Was that you playing drums last night? I thought we were having a thunder storm at first!" He laughed. Resonant. Fun.

"Yeah. It gets all my energy out. I played in band through college."

"Really? Me too! I play flute," I said. A musician. I do like a musician.

"I notice that you go to church on Sundays," I ventured. "Where do you go?"

"I found the little Baptist mission church down the road. It's pretty friendly. Would you like to go with me tomorrow?"

"Sure." I smile, holding on to the fence for support.

"This bathroom is going to be a big job, Jan."

"Yeah, I know. But look how much better it looks now!" The original bathroom was a turn-around-and-sit-down types. We were expanding it by taking out the adjoining closet and doubling the size.

"Let's keep the claw foot bathtub. But how can we take a shower? I don't want to take baths *all* the time," I say.

"They make round rods to hold a surround shower curtain and we could put in a shower, as well" says Rudy. He walks outside to his car to get more tools.

"Have you looked in the paper for other jobs?" I ask.

"Not yet, but Bob, at church, said there's an opening at a place called Bio-Products in Hammond. You know it- it's right down the road from your preschool."

"I guess I have seen it. What do they do there?"

"He says they take fish guts and turn them into pet food- for dogs and cats."

"Wow! Sounds like fun!" I roll my eyes.

"It's got to be better than sassy white sixth graders!" he says. "Jan, I can't teach any more. It stresses me out. By the time I get to school every day my nerves are on edge because I've replayed all the scenarios of back talk and rude comments and mayhem. I'm not where I'm supposed to be in life." He puts down the hammer and sits on the toilet seat. His knuckle goes to his lip as he bites the skin off.

"How much do they pay?" Here it comes.

"I'm not sure, but it's probably not much over minimum wage."

"Do they pay insurance?" I ask. His shoulders are sagging. Here we go again, the defeated persona.

"I don't think so."

"You couldn't try to find another job that would make ends meet?"

"I don't know." His voice is rising. "Maybe *you* should teach in a public school. Your little dream of a preschool doesn't bring in a lot of income. It doesn't have to just be me that all the burden is on!" He gets up and stomps out. I stand, with my arms crossed, and watch him leave. Tell me again why I married this man child?

He *was* right about the preschool. The Philadelphia Preschool, named after the church it was housed in, was growing. I now had eight employees. We were serving families by providing day care for infants through school-age kids. It was my mission to make this the best preschool in the area, developmentally age appropriate, Bible based values, and exceptionally caring and affordable for parents. Being affordable, of course, had the drawbacks of my basically volunteering many months. Maybe I should try to get another job. But I wasn't inclined to give up my dream. Wasn't this what it was like to work on a mission field? Here I could share the gospel daily. I could influence young lives. I could hopefully lead families to church and the truth of God's word. No, this is where God had me. It was up to Howard to figure out where God wanted for him.

CHAPTER **3**

1975

THE GREY SKY encompasses us as Howard and I return from a shopping trip to Flagstaff, Arizona. That's where one went if they wanted to do any serious shopping, something more than what was at the Tuba City Trading Post.

We had enjoyed watching the lightning and listening to the echoing thunder. The windshield wipers can't go fast enough as the rain comes down in torrents and covers the road. When it finally subsides, we inhale the fresh smell of rain in the desert. "It's called petrichor," I say. "It's the word to describe the distinct scent of rain in the air."

"How did you know that?" Howard asks.

"I don't know, I just like the way certain words feel in my mouth. That one just stuck with me. My mom used to teach us an interesting word a day."

Even a small amount of rain brings out the green in the cactus and sage brush. The sun shoots through the clouds in amazing ambers and rose, forming lines illuminating striations of the Painted Desert hills.

"Oh, look, there's a rainbow!" I say.

"Pretty," he says.

"It's just like with Noah, in the Bible," I say.

"That's in the Bible?" he asks.

I laugh. He doesn't know that?

"Of course it's in the Bible. You know, when God makes a promise to never flood the earth again and puts a rainbow in the sky as a sign."

"Do you believe everything in the Bible?" he asks. "I mean, do you really think everything really happened and is true?"

"I believe it could have happened," I say.

"Do you think supernatural things can happen?" he asks.

"Like what?"

"Like, angels or something. A weird thing happened to me last summer, before I met you."

I turn and lean my back on the jeep door so I can give him my full attention. I rest my feet on his driving leg. His eyebrow raises, and he grins.

"I was driving back home from Flagstaff, heading north on the highway," he begins. "You know how there's a dividing cement wall between the north and southbound lanes? Well, there was this guy hitchhiking on the southbound side. I never pick up hitchhikers, but I felt compelled to drive to the next turn around and I drove back and picked this guy up, even though it was the opposite direction from where I was going.

Well, he gets in the jeep and starts asking me things. Things that there is no way he should know. He says, 'Why weren't you drafted?' and 'Your father should never have died from a heart attack.' I never even said anything to him about those things. And get this, he had the most piercing blue eyes I've ever seen. They were, like, they bore right through you."

"He wanted a ride because he said he and his wife and little kid were camping in the arroyo and his car broke down. So, we drove out to where he said it was. We looked for over an hour trying to find the spot where he said he left them. The sun was setting, and the stars were beginning to come out. Finally, we decided to just stay the night out there. I was so scared. Who would leave their wife and little kid in the desert? And who would know all these things about me? I was getting scared and made him walk away about 100 yards from me and sleep there. I could just imagine an ax murderer or something. I couldn't imagine how a woman and her child could survive the heat.

It had to have been 110 degrees."

"The next morning, I woke up at the crack of dawn. I had slept in the jeep and got out to stretch. When I remembered why I was there, I looked everywhere for him, and he was gone! I never saw any sign of him again or of the woman and child. I wonder if he could have been an angel."

We pull up to our little home. It seems like a mansion to me. Our arms are wrapped around grocery bags. Nick runs over from staying next door with Claudia and her son Adam. He dives for Howard's legs and nearly topples him.

"Hey there, little Buddy! How was your day?"

Nick jumps onto the couch. "Fun. I like to play with Adam."

Howard puts down the groceries and finds a Muddy Waters album. He pulls it gently out of the cover and puts the needle on.

"*Sun going down till the moon begins to rise,*
Well I want to rock you baby till you make me satisfied."

He sings along. He comes into the kitchen and pulls me around from where I'm putting groceries away. He leads me in a dance around the room. The walls echo with laughter.

He bends me over backwards and plants a kiss on my lips. I love the taste. He pulls me up. I move in closer and return the favor. He moves his hands to my shoulders and looks into my eyes. I kiss him again. He strokes my cheek with the back of his fingers. I move my hands down his back and slide my fingers into his belt loops. He pulls me closer. I feel the heat rising.

I pull away and put my hands on his shoulders.

"Do you really think we need to follow everything in the Bible?" I ask.

"Like what? Yeah, if it's in the New Testament," he says.

"Like, where it says fornicators won't go to heaven in 1 Corinthians," I say.

"What does that even mean?" he asks.

I walk over to the bookshelf and pull out the dictionary.

"Fornicator," I read. "Voluntary sexual relations between two persons or two persons not married to each other."

Howard sits down on the couch. I sit beside him and slide my hand in his. He shakes his head.

"Maybe we better stop until we get married," he says. "We can wait two months."

I nod and lay my head on his shoulder knowing that it will not be easy to stop what we've begun.

"Where should we get married?" Howard asks. He's just hung up the phone from calling Lucie, his mom and telling her the news.

"What did she say?" I ask.

"She thinks it's a little soon in our relationship to be making wedding plans. Do you think we're rushing things?" he asks.

"I don't know. We've been together every day for four months. That's the longest relationship I've ever had!" I say.

I pick up a dishtowel and begin drying the dishes.

Am I rushing things? I think. He goes to church, he plays an instrument, he's a teacher like me, he is cute, he's good with Nick. Well, mostly good considering he's never had kids before.

"I guess we should get married in Scottsdale. I don't really know anyone here. Who do you think will come?" I say.

"My mom, I guess. I have an aunt and cousin in Glendale."

"We could ask my youth pastor, Brian to marry us." I think about how he and his wife took me in for a few months when I was single and pregnant with Nick my last year of college. My mom didn't know what to do with me. I had been so afraid to tell her I was pregnant. I had gone to my great aunt Betty and told her, asking her if she would tell my mom for me. She wasn't about to take on my responsibility and made sure I knew that that was my job.

I didn't really relish the idea of telling Mom that Jim was really just a guy I met at the amusement park where I was working as at the concessions stand. He *was* pretty cute- blonde hair, blue eyes, high cheekbones. We went out a couple of times and then he brought me flowers. I thought I had died and gone to heaven. No one had ever brought me flowers before. The several dates ended up in his bedroom. Why wouldn't I want to sleep with him? Everyone slept around. And I hadn't yet realized how I grieved God by those decisions.

It did bother me a little that his best friend wouldn't let anyone take photos of him. And there was that one night at a party where they were passing around joints and some little white tablet. I managed to pass that on without being noticed. But, hey, he was really cute, with his blond hair and green eyes. And he brought me flowers.

I wasn't talking to my mom much. I just didn't know what to say. She had flown Jim from Chicago, where he moved back with his family, to try and help me see the light, that "a baby should have a name". I was embarrassed to see Jim, because when I had called him on the pay phone and told him I was pregnant, all he said was, "How do I know it's mine?" There was no doubt that the baby was his. I hadn't slept with anyone else.

My visit with my dad ended up by him telling me not to expect him to contribute to my bastard child. Mom would offer a few bits of advice on my pregnancy, like, *you need a bigger bra*, or *those stretch marks will be there till you die*. She just figured if I got myself into this mess, I should be adult enough to get myself to doctor appointments at the clinic and figure out the details. She pawned me off on Pastor Keith and his wife Terri who had an extra room. I remembered sitting around their dinner table, making polite conversation. Terri showed me exercises to do that she assured me would make for an easier delivery. I guess the exercises worked. How would I know? This was my first baby.

"Yeah, that sounds good," Howard says. "And get married in your old church?"

"I guess so."

Books and movies seem to have characters putting in a lot more thought and planning into a union that should be for life than what Howard and I did. I walked down the aisle with a teal crepe dress. The pleated bodice and thousands of covered buttons took hours to make using my sister's treadle sewing machine. I would have loved a Cinderella white wedding dress, but white was out of the question as I was "soiled" and no longer pure. Little Nick preceded me with rose petals. Howard looked amazing in his deep teal wool suit, which his mom had purchased for him. I gazed into his blue eyes as Pastor Keith read the vows. Howard placed my grandmother's wedding ring on my finger. I placed his grandfather's ring on his.

The potluck reception was held in my Aunt Betty's back yard. January was a perfect month to be surrounded by cactus and Olive trees. Having my family and Lucie there to enjoy our celebration was just right.

CHAPTER 4

1976
Tuba City, Arizona

"LOOK AT THIS one! It must have come from a large pot. Look at all the cool designs they painted," Howard says. Nick and I turn to look with amazement. The spring air is fresh. We are digging in the dirt on the side of a hill not far from our house in Tuba City, Arizona. We're not sure if this was a ceremonial site, hopefully we're not intruding. A fellow teacher had told us about this place. Nick puts another paint chard into his box. He picks up his little shovel and digs again.

"Oh....my.... gosh!" he exclaims. "Look at this!" he holds up an arrow head.

"You found an arrow head?" Howard grins and gives him a hug. "We're just like archaeologists." Nick smiles proudly, loving to use "big" words.

The sun is starting to set. The rays are hitting the painted hills creating rich purples and magentas. Nick tries to lift the box with both hands, but it starts to fall. I reach out and grab it before we climb into the jeep and drive the few miles home.

Once inside the kitchen, I open a can of refried beans, spread it on tortillas, top with shredded cheese and pop them in the oven.

"How long do you think we should stay here, in Tuba City?" I ask. The year is coming to an end. We should start thinking about what we're doing for next year. Our contracts are coming up for renewal.

"I don't know, don't you like it here?" Howard replies.

"I do, but it's so isolated. Do you think this is where we want to raise our kids?"

"I kinda like it here. The students are really great and well behaved. They would be good friends for Nick. I do *not* ever want to live in a big city again. Los Angeles was way too big and impersonal."

"I don't know. It just seems like there would be a lot more experiences and things available to Nick if we moved to a larger town. I don't want to live in a huge city either. Phoenix was big enough to be swallowed alive!" I say.

"I've always wanted to live in a commune," Howard says.

"A commune?"

"Yeah, you know, like in the Bible in Acts where they all joined everything they owned and lived off the land."

"What would that be like, I mean, would we not own anything? Everything would be shared?"

"I'm not sure." Howard goes to the desk and pulls out a pamphlet he's been saving for such a time as this. "Look at this!" We sit down on the couch together. It's a black and white copy machine tri-fold with some hazy pictures of people sitting and eating together at a long camp table in a cabin. Another photo is of people working out in a communal garden with hoes and wheelbarrows. The women are wearing dresses and head scarves. The men have suspenders. The heading says,

Highway Missionary Society
Life as God Intended

"Where is this place, anyways?" I ask. Howard turns the brochure over. *Located in God's Country, near Jacksonville, Oregon.*

In May, we both resign our teaching jobs, pack up all our belongings, rent a U-Haul truck and start driving. We find ourselves in Colorado, driving through unbelievably majestic Rocky Mountain peaks. We camp in Durango, Silverton and Grand Junction. We go to the parks and eavesdrop on conversations. We drive around looking at churches. We walk down the sidewalks and window shop. Beautiful? Yes, but they just don't feel right.

"Where else should we try?" Howard asks.

"I don't know. I remember how much my sibs and I liked Oregon when my parents would go there to study in the summers. And it was nice and green when I lived there. The ocean is nearby. There's actually rain! Do you want to try that?"

We head to the coast and drive up Hwy 101.

"Tell me what your dreams for life are," I ask as we drive the windy road.

"Wow, that's a little deep don't you think?" Howard asks.

"Yeah, I guess, but I really want to know."

"Well, let's see. I guess I want to live as simple a lifestyle as possible. I would love to live in the country in a log cabin."

"I tried that. It was ok, I guess, but I'm not sure that's what I want to do forever."

"I would love to just be able to be apart from the "dog-eat-dog" world. Really, I will never be completely happy until I get to heaven."

"Which won't be for a very long time!"

"He grins. Sure hope not! My main dream would be to live in the country and not be in perpetual debt. I would like to have an outdoor job- I would love to be a farmer. I would have to build up my endurance!"

I look at his skinny arms and picture him behind a plow.

"I don't want to be associated with teaching all my life." He passes a slow-moving RV. "I wouldn't mind being a missionary and helping people build ditches as long as I was helping them in practical things that they needed and desired. As a teacher I feel like I am just in a continual struggle. I would like to work with adults, however, who sought me to help them."

"What do you want to do?" he asks me.

"All I've ever wanted to do was to run a preschool. I love working with little kids. When I was in college, I volunteered at a Head Start and loved it. Then I worked at a preschool in Scottsdale. Someone there told me they thought I would be a good director. I guess that really planted the seed," I said.

"When I was in college, I wanted to go to the Indian Reservation and teach. I got all the Bureau of Indian Affairs circulars and mailed away to them even as I was a junior in college. I wanted to get away from Los Angeles, for one thing," Howard said.

We stop at a viewpoint in Cannon Beach. Haystack Rock protrudes majestically from the ocean. We'll have to stop there when we have more time.

"I also wanted to teach people who really needed dedicated teachers and were happy to have them. I wanted to teach Indians because I felt they were the most downtrodden people in the country. I wanted to help the downtrodden. Once I was there, I relished the simple lifestyle."

We end up in Hammond, Oregon, and camp at Ft. Stevens State Park. We are awestruck at the beauty. We can barely see the tops of the majestic Cedar trees. We haul out our bikes and ride the many trails to the beach and lake. And oh, the fragrance of the pines and fresh outdoors. The blue jay's melodies are pure happiness.

Sunday, we find a small church a few miles away from the park. Surrounded by friendly people, we are enraptured by the worship. The freedom to lift our hands in praise. The rich teaching. We looked at each other and lock eyes. I think we found our place! After the service ends, I ask Pastor Dennis, "Does there happen to be a need for a preschool around here?"

"Oh, absolutely! The nearest day care is in Astoria, half an hour away."

That is all the encouragement I need. We make the decision then and there to make this our new home.

A year later, after much intricate, detailed planning, I am able to begin a very successful preschool and day care in the church.

Sing-a-long and morning devotions is over, and I return to my office. Dorothy has her head buried in the books, her short, frosted hair shines as a beam of sunshine strikes it through the window. The phone rings. She stops and picks it up.

"Philadelphia Preschool. Yes, we still have openings. Sure, come on in this morning. We'd love to meet you." She looks at me.

"Another four-year-old." I smile. Dorothy had been my faithful secretary for five years. She'd been there through thick and thin, since the beginning, really. She set up the books, gave advice on hiring, worked with the board. She has encouraged me and been a firm foundation. And best of all, she prays with me every day.

"How are we doing on the finances?" I ask.

"Looks like you'll get paid this month!" She grins. She knows this is not always the case.

"I'm sure glad. We really need it." Dorothy picks up a pencil with her slender hands and continues writing in the ledger.

Howard walks through the door. "I'm going home with Dennis. He'll drop me off. Do you want me to take Sara and Kyle?"

"Sure, I'll be home around three." I give him a peck on his bearded cheek. He takes Sara's small hand as Kyle runs ahead to Dennis' car. I watch them drive away. It's nice to have him take them so I could get some uninterrupted work done. Besides, it's good "daddy" time. He'd read them stories and play games.

I sit down at my desk and begin to read the mail. Suddenly I look up.

"Dorothy, are the keys hanging on the rack?" She gets up and looks.

"Yes!" Her eyes are bright, quizzical.

"Howard will have a hard time getting into the house without the keys! He'll be calling." I shake my head. It's just like him to forget something important like that.

Half an hour later the phone rings.

"Philadelphia Preschool." I answer.

"I figured you'd call." I smile.

I WILL ENTER HIS GATES

"What?" I cover the receiver with my hand. "Dorothy, can you check the coat rack and see if my keys are there?" She arches her eyebrows, looking at me like I've lost a screw, but walks over there anyway.

"The keys are gone," she says. I look at her and frown.

"Did you move my keys?" I ask.

"No- haven't touched them."

I uncover the receiver. "Howard, how did you get into the house? No way. No way! No way." I hang up the phone and sit on the edge of my desk, my hands clasp the smooth cold ledge. I shake my head in disbelief.

"What happened?" Dorothy asks. She turns her swivel chair to look at me. I'm sitting there with my mouth slightly open and shake my head again. My brows are furrowed. "I can't believe it!"

"What *happened*?" she repeats.

"Howard got home and realized he didn't have the keys. So, he took Sara to look for an open window. He hoisted her onto his shoulders, so she could reach the kitchen window. It was open. When she started moving the plants, so she could get through, she said, 'Here Daddy, here's your keys.' And she hands him the keys! The keys that are no longer on the coat rack! They're the same keys!"

Dorothy's mouth drops open incredulously. "Are you sure they're not there?" she asks.

"You just checked!" I laugh, shaking my head.

Howard's Journal
JANUARY 12

A most unusual thing happened today. Dennis took Sara, Kyle and me to go home and when we got there, I realized I forgot the house key. We started searching for open windows and I hoisted Sara up to the kitchen window. She slid it open and said, "Daddy, are these your keys?" I feel like God is telling me that there will come a time in the near future when He will be opening a door for me where there is no way out. He will provide the keys!

CHAPTER 5

1978
Hammond, Oregon

*Heaven is a wonderful place
Filled with Glory and Grace
I want to see my Savior's face
Cuz heaven is a wonderful place
I wanna go there...*

I WATCH THOSE cherubic little faces singing. Twenty of them seated on the carpet, legs criss- cross applesauce, hands dutifully in their laps.

"Teacher Jan." Carlita is waving her hand in the air. "Teacher Jan, if Heaven is so wonderful, why don't people just kill themselves so they can go there?"

I touch her smooth, brown chin. Her charcoal eyes are intent. "Heaven *is* a wonderful place," I say, "But we have to wait until Jesus decides it's time for us to go there. If a person killed themselves to get there sooner, the rest of us would be soooo sad. Your mommy and daddy would be sad. Your brothers and sisters would be sad."

"Not *my* brother!" says Danielle. She scrunches up her face. "He is stupid, mean and nasty!"

"Oh yes he would. And most of all, I would be sad. I would miss you."

I WILL ENTER HIS GATES

Cuz heaven is a wonderful
Heaven is a wonderful
Heaven is a wonderful place.

We finish singing and watch as all the three and four-year-olds line up and follow their teachers to their classrooms.

Having my own preschool was all I had ever wanted to do. When I was in high school, I had seen a sign advertising for Head Start volunteers. I had signed up and was enraptured by little people. What could be more fun than this? Hanging out with kids who said ridiculously funny things, getting to read fantasies, filling my days with imagination and cuddles.

I had begun college at Arizona State University with a degree in Art. I had been surrounded by artists growing up. I was creative. It seemed like a good choice at the time. And I definitely, absolutely did not want to be a teacher. My mom was a teacher, my dad was a teacher. My aunts were teachers. But two years into it, I realized that working with little kids made my heart sing. I changed my major to Early Childhood Education.

A month before my college graduation, without a job prospect and looking for adventure and connection, I wrote a letter to my friend Kathy asking if I could visit her home in the rural Pacific Northwest. Kathy and I had met the first summer my parents had gone to Eugene to study. She lived next door and we had become fast friends, going to the pool every day, trips to the library, hiking the many trails. Over the years we had written back and forth until college when we drifted apart. The last I had heard, she had married and moved to a small log cabin near a stream in the woods.

After visiting, she convinced me to move there. I loaded up a small U-Haul trailer with my tangerine, sleek Danish couch which I had received from my mom for a graduation present, my bed, my photos, a crib and a few toys and books for Nick.

When I arrived, Kathy and her husband Keith told me about a little hunting shack that I could rent for $20 a month. There was no electricity or running water, but it was beside a creek and I could get water from there. Who really thought about what animals had been in it or what anyone might be putting into it, including washing their clothes and dishes.

The two small rooms were enough for a four-month old and me. The couch fit easily in the eight-foot living room. The old yellow stove was heated by a propane bottle. I went to the hardware store and purchased a kerosene lantern, so I had some light at night.

The hardware store became my best friend. I learned how to take PVC pipe and lay it on the hill for a gravity feed water system, which I hooked to the sink.

Winter came and with it snow. Such a rare experience for me having grown up in Arizona. When the large, fluffy flakes began to fall, white against the grey sky, I grabbed Nick and we looked out the window.

"Look, Nick, it's snow. Let's go outside and play in it."

He pointed and babbled. I bundled him up in a blanket and we stood outside looking up and lifting our faces to the sky. The cold flakes landed softly in our hair and faces. Nick giggled.

It snowed all night. The next morning my car had a foot of snow covering it. We delighted in the blanket of white that covered the fields and trees. The pine branches bent beneath the weight of the snow. The indigo of a Blue Jay was a colorful contrast to the vast whiteness.

Those moments of delight turned into days of trying to stay warm. I turned on the oven and kept the door open, standing near with outstretched hands. It was probably not the wisest choice, but it was what was available. It was the only heat in the cabin.

I kept a gallon jar beside my bed to pee in. If I had to use the outhouse, which consisted of a hole in the ground with a platformed box for sitting on, I took two of Nick's cloth diapers and folded them up to lay beside the hole so that I had something to sit on. That, of course, was after I had brushed the snow off the sides. Maybe I should figure out how to build a house around this poor excuse for a bathroom.

Having no shower at the house, I went every other day to a community shower. It was a small wood cabin with four spigots which were arranged along one wall. Water piped through a wood stove heated the shower. The first day I closed my eyes as I let the hot water stream through my long hair. When I opened them, I was shocked to see a gangly, long-haired young man pull his clothes off and take his place at the spigot beside me.

"You new around here?" he asked.

I turned my back to him, embarrassed as I quickly scrubbed my body and said, "Yes, I live near Kathy."

"Oh, great gal. Let me know if you need anything!"

I mumbled a thank you and quickly grabbed my towel and made a speedy retreat.

The bright green tips of the giant fir trees were budding. Purple Crocuses were peeking out of the new field grass. The days were becoming warmer. I was missing my friends in Scottsdale. I was missing the sun streaming down on me, warming me to my insides. I was missing having a purpose. I packed up my few belongings, padded the back seat of my yellow Duster with blankets to try and keep Nick safe and headed south.

Two days of long driving later, I could see the thousands of bright lights of Phoenix ahead. Up till the outskirts, the inky black sky held radiant brilliant stars. The Big Dipper was easy to spot, Orion's Belt, the North Star. Back home.

CHAPTER 6

Warrenton

TODDLER TEARS FROM the neighboring bedroom awaken me. I look at the clock. Six a.m. O.K. Here we go. It's gonna be a long day. I crawl out of bed and make my way into Kyle's room. He's standing up in his crib. Tears are running down his rosy cheeks. His white blonde hair, chicken fuzz we call it, stands straight up. His arms are raised anticipating my rescue.

"Good morning doll. How was your sleep? Ready for a new day?" He nuzzles into my neck. I take him back to my bed to nurse him. Howard reaches over to stroke Kyle's arm.

"How are ya, Little Blessing?" he asks. Kyle reaches his free arm to explore Howard's beard. Howard sits up and stretches, then suddenly proclaims, "Hey! I've been healed! Jan," he sits up and looks around, "my eyes have been healed! God has healed my eyes! I can see!" I look over at him, surprised. Howard has the worst eyesight ever. His glasses, thick as Coke bottles, are always the first thing he puts on in the morning.

He hops out of bed, looking around the room. He goes to the window and looks out. "Wow! Would you look at those trees! They're so clear!" He's wearing a huge grin. He heads to the bathroom. Kyle's done nursing. He slides off the bed and toddles off to wake his sister. Howard returns to the bedroom. His smile is gone. Shoulders slumped.

"I left my contacts in overnight," he says. I feel bad for him. I reach over and touch his hand.

"But God could heal your eyes. You know that, right?" I ask. He nods imperceptibly.

This walk. This journey. So many highs and lows. Learning to redefine ourselves into who we are in Christ. Learning who this Jesus is. What our expectations are of Him. What His expectations are of us. Just when you think you're getting it figured out, there's a whoop-de-doo.

I dress and go into the living room and sit on the couch. Thank goodness for Lucie's hand-me-down-furniture. Kyle and Sara climb onto my lap. I pull the lap quilt I just finished making over them. I love this time. The cuddling. The reflecting. Thanksgiving has come and gone and now it's time to think of Christmas. Howard and I have had lengthy discussions of what is the "right" way to celebrate Christmas. Is it ok to have a tree? Weren't they from a pagan influence? Should we do Santa? That takes away from the real reason for Christmas, right? Or maybe we could incorporate both. Can we be careful to be "in the world" to celebrate and still be mindful of Christ's birth?

We've decided we want to make as many gifts as we can. We've decided on homemade, dipped candles, cheese, book marks, and ornaments. Anything should be made inexpensively and cost little to send. It shouldn't require a great deal of time either but should show thought and love. If we do cheese, we should start this weekend, so it has time to age. And whatever we do should include the kids in making it.

"I'm hungry," Sara says.

Kyle's head pops up. "Pancakes," he says.

Sara runs into the kitchen and starts pulling out a bowl and pancake mix. Kyle scoots the little stool over.

"I help too," he says.

Howard is just coming down the driveway where he has gone to "walk and pray", a daily routine. I pull a plate out and put the stack of pancakes on the table. Howard comes in, excitement on his face.

"Jan," he says. He turns me towards him and puts his hands on my shoulders. "It's grace!"

"OK," I say. He must have had another revelation. I set the syrup on the table.

"God just revealed to me that it's by grace we've been saved! It's not works. I've been saved by grace! Do you realize how great that is?"

"Yeah, of course. You didn't know that?" I ask.

"Boy howdie! I never knew. I never realized. I thought I had to do all these things in order for Him to love and accept me. This is why I have to walk and pray every day."

I pat him on the shoulder placatingly and put the silverware on the table. He heads to his desk and pulls out his journal and pen.

Ephesians 2:8
For by grace you have been saved and that not of yourselves, it is the gift of God.

I just realized that this is true! I never knew! I thought I had to be good and pray and do good things for people in order to get to heaven. But that's not what the Bible says. It's a free gift! It's right here in my hands.

Once we come under grace under Jesus' wings, we are to willingly cast off the old man of sin and begin to absorb God's perfect law- love and the law cannot be separated. One and the same being gave them both. We may fail, but that doesn't mean that we shouldn't strive all the harder to be pleasing to God's law. God's son- Jesus- leads us to God's law. There is no threat if we fail, but one must be diligent to try to observe the law. We are not just under grace without the law, but too, we are not under the law without grace. Only we have God's mercy when we fail; nonetheless, we are striving to meet the conditions of God's law. God is Jesus; Jesus is God. You can't have one without the other- they are compliments.

God is not just out there, a righteous standard to be kept. You are dealing not only with God, but with Jesus too. And the Holy Spirit. I was dealing separately with each one, and I had to have infallible proof of their existence before I would give wholehearted commitment. I was whole heartedly committed to Jesus, but not the other two. I realized that the Lord your God is one God. Made up of a trinity. One God who reveals himself in the different ways. It's a whole lot easier to deal with one God rather than three individual Gods.

CHAPTER 7

Warrenton

"LOOK! SARA, KYLE! Come look out the window!" Nick calls. I come into the living room where they are piled up on their knees on the couch looking out the window.

"It's snowing!" he says.

"Yay!" Sara shouts. "We can go make a snowman! We can go sled down the driveway!"

Snow is indeed falling. This is such a rare thing for us. Rain? Yes. Snow, seldom. We watch it drift down in clumps, covering the ground.

"Did you know that God made each snowflake unique and special?" I ask.

"He did?"

Howard joins us.

"Yeah, each and every one is different. If you look under a microscope you can see how they are each uniquely formed," he says. We are mesmerized watching it. So soft. So encompassing.

"Can we go out in it?" Sara asks.

"Sure! Get your coats!" Howard helps Kyle on with his coat and boots and little gloves. They scramble off and are ready in short order, running over each other to get outside.

"Looks like we'll have a white Christmas after all," he says, pulling on his jacket.

"I'll get the hot cocoa going," I say. "You'll be wanting some

I WILL ENTER HIS GATES

warming up when you return."

Pour some milk in a pan I stir in some cocoa and sugar. I put it on low on the stove. I start to tidy up. I turn on the Christmas lights. Straighten the shoes, fold the couch blanket, tidy up Howard's desk. Hey, what's this? A letter to Lucie for Christmas.

Mom,

This is really going to be an old-fashioned Christmas- I'm going to tell you what we need! This is the first time I have communicated on the subject ever. I always say, "I don't know," or "I don't care." Well, not this year. Well, anyway, the needs:

Howard: Pay off Old Testament and new testament tape sets

Vitamins C, Potassium, Calcium, Therma M multi-vitamin, compact cassette player (play-tapes)

Jan: clothes; scissors- good pair of sewing scissors

Nick- winter coat; alternatives: from Toys to Grow on catalog- Hide out bed tent; Lego kit, from JC Penny catalog- anything from GI Joe pages 4-84 especially cobra water moccasin

Sara: Last 4 reading institute kits, long sleeve turtle neck, pink size 5

Experiments in aerospace

Kyle- Dinosaurs (Giant flexible)

Presents of Nick and Howard are merely alternatives; Jan needs school clothes, Sara needs turtle necks and we need for the Reading Institute to be paid off; and Kyle would really like to have the "monsters" Nick has gotten very little over the past years from us and we would like to see him overjoyed for once.

How are the arrangements for the trip coming?

Did he tell me he wrote this? He must have made a copy, so he'd remember what he asked for. Lucie will be coming for Christmas. I guess she'll have an extra-large suitcase. I always look forward to her coming, mixed with a little dread. Whenever she writes, Howard leaves the letter on his desk for a week before he opens it. She knows how to say what's on her mind with a mix of manipulation. Her letters and conversations always start innocently enough but end up with criticism or something to make you feel guilty. Hopefully this will be a fun time. The kids always enjoy her doting over them at any rate.

I look up as I hear stomping by the front door. They must be getting cold. I stash the letter back into the pile and head to the stove to ladle the chocolate.

"Was it fun?" I ask.

"I'm cold!" Sara wraps her arms around herself and shivers.

"Well, let's get that coat off. Let me help you with those boots." Sara climbs onto a chair at the table.

"Hey, did you hear that?" she asks.

"No, did you hear something?"

"Stop, listen. There it is again," she says.

"What is it?" Nick asks. "Hey, I hear it. I think it's over here. It sounds like a rat."

I am hoping he's not right. Nick and Sara go into the living room, looking for hidden treasure. He stops.

"Over here- it's under the Christmas tree."

I go in to take a look. Nick grabs the backpack that's under the tree. It's an old one that's been laying around. Why it's under the tree, I'm not sure. Nick starts to unzip it.

"Nooooo!!" Kyle screams and tries to grab it away.

"Mine present." He takes it and runs to his room with it. We all follow along. "Go away. It's for Christmas," he says.

I wave everyone out of the room and sit down on the floor by him.

"What's in it, honey?" I ask.

"Mine!" he says.

"Let me see, sweetie. I won't tell anyone," I say. I pry off his death grip. I hear something clawing around inside.

I slowly unzip it and inside is our pet Guinea pig.

"Alrighty then," I say. "Kyle, you can't wrap up a Guinea pig. They won't live in there. It was really nice of you to want to give a present, but this is really not good for the Guinea pig." I take it out of the backpack and let him hold it. He cuddles it and kisses its head.

Laughter rings out from the hall. His siblings have been eavesdropping.

"Go on now," I shoo them. "Go drink your cocoa," I say.

CHAPTER 8

Howard's Journal
August 20, 1983

Working at Bioproducts, I find myself digging fish guts out of the drain. I feel that I am better than all that. I rebel at the thought. I can't cut the mustard. But, only one who can dig fish guts out of the drain happily is ready for service to the Lord. One who recognizes that he has no rights at all is ready for service. I fall short. One who wished to let sin enter the world through him will have many trials and testings. But when he learns to release anger by crying out through prayer rather than by releasing hostility in any other way, he is approaching the way of the cross.

When we can say "I don't want to do that, but I must do that, he is headed on the road of discipleship. He is learning to humble himself in each and every various situation he faces. He is learning the way of the cross.

ANOTHER DAY, ANOTHER dollar. Some days you just couldn't win. I'm driving my blue Suburu hatchback home from the preschool. An SUV comes whizzing past me, on me before I can even see it in my rearview mirror and cuts it so close to me that I can feel my car shake with the wind it creates. I suppress the urge to flip him off. I do allow myself a "damn, don't you know I've got kids in the car??"

I had had an unusually high amount of calls today wanting drop-in care for infants. How could I say no? Each child was so much more per hour and we were always tight at the end of the month. I had overloaded the infant/ toddler room. I was only supposed to have eight kids. At one point in the day we had fifteen. I was not on the best-boss-award list today. I had helped out when I could, but apparently, that wasn't enough. By the end of the day, Allison had had enough and quit.

I had gone to the file cabinet in my office and pulled out a stack of applications I kept in a just-in-case file. It was really hard to find employees that were Christian, had child care experience and wanted part-time work. The only real benefit I offered was allowing employees to bring their children to work, which, after all, was a pretty good perk if you had a baby or preschooler. And Hammond wasn't exactly a convenient location. Well, I'd just pray about it. God always came through in a pinch.

I pull into the graveled driveway, walk around and undo Kyle's seatbelt. Sara undoes hers by herself and slides out of the car. I walk into the house with Kyle on my hip and deposit him on the floor along with the diaper bag and my purse. Nick was already home. I had been allowing him to be home alone when it was just a few hours or so. He was, after all, nine and that was allowable by law and I knew he'd only be home alone for a half an hour.

"Where's daddy?" I ask him.

"Out walking and praying." Nick says.

"Ok. How was your day?"

"Not so good." He's sitting on the floor playing with his GI Joes.

"What happened not so good?" I ask.

He picks up a GI Joe and starts making shooting sounds aiming at another one. I go sit beside him on the floor.

"What happened?" I ask again.

"That kid pushed me again today. I tried to get out of his way, but he pushed me."

"What did your teacher do?"

"She didn't know."

"You didn't tell her?"

"He said if I told he'd give me more than a shove." I put my arm around him.

"I'll call her tomorrow." I said.

I hear the front door close. I look up and see Howard. He's walking with a limp. Hmmmm. I see he needs a haircut. His straight hair is hanging in his eyes. I better get out the scissors.

"How was your day? Please tell me it was good. I'm not really in the mood for any more bad things," I say.

"Uhhhhh," he says.

"You're limping," I say.

"Yeah. So about that. I fell at work today. I don't know what happened, just was like my leg buckled out from under me and I fell."

"Did anyone see you?"

"Yeah, but they're hoping I don't claim a Workman's Comp on it. They wanted me to see how it went. It's a little better, but I'm not so sure."

"Maybe you should call the chiropractor and make an appointment," I say.

"Yeah, could you do that for me tomorrow?"

I roll my eyes. Can't he make his own appointments?

Howard hobbles into the living room and picks up his concertina. He loves Irish music and has figured out how to play Amazing Grace, Old Time Religion and When the Saints Go Marching In. Hearing him play renews joy and calmness to the room. It makes me remember what I loved about him when I married him. His creativity. His love of music. That love of music and wanting to minister had led him and several others to form a Christian band called Just As We Are. Highway Missionary Society's band Servant were their role models. Keith Green, Leon Patillo, Andrae Crouch and 2nd Chapter of Acts were some of the few Christian artists at the time. Janet and Grant Larson, Alan Yankus and Howard lined up bookings at other churches and played. They not only played locally but went as far as Seattle, Washington. From that ministry grew a Street Theater Troupe. I joined them, and we would perform at the mall in Longview, Washington, in front of the Liberty Theater in Astoria and on the Prom in Seaside. After we would perform our skit, we would give a testimony and pray with anyone who wanted it.

Real, raw, bold ministry. Yes, even on bad days, you had to come back to what you were meant to be.

CHAPTER 9

Warrenton

"HOW WAS YOUR day?" I ask Howard as he takes off his smelly, fishy boots. I take out a pan and fill it with water for a box of mac and cheese.

"It was ok. Bioproducts isn't the best job in the world. The guys I work with are pretty worldly. Mostly I just read my Bible during lunch. I don't really want to participate in their conversations." Howard is leaning against the counter, arms crossed.

"Like what do they want to talk about?" I ask. I begin making a salad. He grabs a knife from the drawer and begins cutting carrots.

"Oh, I don't know. Like one guy was talking about a movie he saw the other night about a couple who was having an affair and how funny it was. Or about going to the bar and getting so drunk they could hardly drive home. Stuff like that. I just don't fit into that. And I don't want to. Was there any mail today?" he asks.

"Just a letter from your mom. And some bills."

Howard opens the bills.

"What?" he yells. "The bank has the statement wrong. Again! Can't they ever get it right?"

I look over his shoulder, holding my wet hands in the air.

"They charged an overdraft on the house payment check! I just put money in the bank. There should have been enough to cover it." He throws the statement onto the counter. "Why is the burden of proof

I WILL ENTER HIS GATES

always on me? If I call them up, they're just gonna make some lame excuse as to why they're right. I *hate* living in the world. Everyone is always out to get you." He goes into the living room and plops down on the couch. I know this isn't the time to bring it up, but I have to.

"Howard, um, we need to talk about the car." I dry my hands and throw the towel on the counter. "It's been leaking fluid onto the passenger side. I'm not sure what it is, but it can't be good," I say. "And the fan belt is screeching every time I start the car."

He holds his head in his hands. "I'm not a mechanic! What do I know about fixing cars?"

"I don't know anything either, but something has to be done! I can't continue to drive to work every day with it limping along. It's not safe for me or the kids. It's like you don't even care," I say.

"We don't have money to fix cars," he says looking up.

"Well then, you should have thought about that before you went and quit your teaching job that had a good salary and benefits!" I say, my voice rising.

He stands up and heads down the hall to the bathroom. I follow him in there.

"I had to quit. It was too stressful," he says.

"But you could have thought about your family first," I say. My tone is acid.

He's fuming. He kicks the toilet. We hear a crack. Water begins to rush onto the floor. I shake my head. What the heck? I grab a towel and start mopping it up.

"Now look what you've done. We'll have to pay someone to come fix it with the money we don't have to fix the car," I say. Howard stomps off.

"I should have just found a cabin in the woods to live in where there weren't any problems!" He slams the door and walks out. I follow him to the living room. We need to talk. Now!

Howard is pacing. I sit down on the orange couch that Lucie had handed down to us. I sit cross legged. My arms are crossed.

"This, this thing that you call marriage, is not working. You can't ever seem to get a grip on the realities of life. Paying bills on time, keeping a job, holding up your end of the bargain," I spew. Howard bites his lip and keeps pacing. I continue, like a machine gun. "When are you going to grow up? When are you going to realize that everyone is not out to get you? That you have to roll with the punches? That you have to be the one to change your circumstances to fit the world? You're so heavenly minded you're no earthly good! 'I need time to pray. I need time to read the Bible and journal,' I mimic sarcastically. "Meanwhile who's holding everything together? Me! That's who! I don't respect you. I need a man who can be there for me. For the kids. Who can take care of us and our needs."

Howard sits down on the opposite chair. His head is in his hands. "I know, Jan. I know I'm not the husband you hoped for. But what are you suggesting? That we get a divorce?"

There, he's said it so it's out in the open. No, I don't want a divorce. But I'm not sure I can continue living this way. My parents were divorced. I know what it's like to be a kid growing up without a dad. It's not fun. Would I choose that for my kids? And what does the Bible say? "God hates divorce." In a lot of ways being divorced would be easier. I'd just continue doing what I'm doing now, only without the tension. But could I face my friends, family, the church and let them know that we failed?

"I don't know. I just know we need a change." I feel that lump forming in my throat. "Maybe we should go to counseling or something," I say softly.

"Yeah, maybe. I'm not sure if I'm cut out for that," he says. He stands up. "I'm going to walk and pray."

I head to our bedroom and fall face down on my bed, sobbing. Why can't he be someone who takes care of us? Maybe I should never have married him. I continue to sob uncontrollably. What is going on with me? What is the real issue here, God? Howard is trying the best he can, for whatever that's worth.

Suddenly, I get a vision of my dad leaving us. I'm thirteen. My brother, sisters and I are shocked. My parents never fought. We had no idea there was a problem between them. My dad never sat us down and told us anything. Just there one day and gone the next.

The light is beginning to dawn on me. I was abandoned, wasn't I, Lord? He wasn't there to provide for us or make us feel safe or be a role model.

A new vision appears. My college French teacher. He was forty-one. I was eighteen. He asked me one day if I would come to his house to help with Boy Scouts. I said I'd be glad to. He gave me his address and I went over the next week. I met his son and wife. He was from the Isle of Mann in England and she was British as well. It was fun helping out and being needed. He asked me to return the following week. This time, his wife and son were gone. And this time, there was no Boy Scouts meeting. What's going on here, I thought. Why am I here if not to help with the kids? We talked casually for a while, him boasting about the satanic cults on the Isle. Then he approached me and began kissing me. What should I do? He was older than me and I was to respect adults, right? But this was wrong. I had no real desire to be with him, but he started telling me about how, when he looked at me in class, all he thought about was how beautiful I was and how great my French accent was. The next thing I knew, he had me in his bedroom, stripped and vulnerable. I was scared. I wanted to get away, but I didn't know how.

After I returned home, I felt so ashamed. I couldn't tell my mom. What would she say? We had never talked about sex or relationships. And now I had to go to French class and face him. Again.

I continued to see him twice more. I felt like I had to do whatever he wanted. He was, after all, my professor, and older than I.

I met him at the college where he told me to get in his white pickup. We drove North for a couple of hours until he pulled over on a side road. I took slow, small bites of the sandwich he offered me. I felt so vulnerable. I knew this wasn't right, but what could I do? Now I was out in the middle of nowhere and nowhere to run or get away. He led me to the back of his pickup where he laid out a blanket and began to take off my clothes.

When I had come home, I sobbed, overcome with guilt. How could I be involved in this? God, how do I get out of this? How can You love me when I'm in the midst of this? What would his wife think? Or do to me if she found out? I resolved to drop out of the class and avoid all further phone calls.

God, this is so painful. Why are you dredging all this up in me? What purpose can there be?

Jan, I love you, He whispers. *I was there all along. I am your husband, your provider, your lover. I will never leave you or forsake you. I will always be there for you. I've vindicated you.*

Peace. Unimaginable peace settles over me.

Howard's Letter
NOVEMBER 4, 1984
Jan,

You don't know the inner restlessness, turmoil, anxiety, and frustration I am going through working three jobs. I have had no quality prayer life for the past four weeks. I need to go out, sit down, close my eyes, and pour my heart out before the Lord with no time limit. I haven't done this but once or twice for the last month.

For me today, the answer was not praying with my family or you until I could get all the inner turmoil out of my life. I decided I wanted to go pray by myself while I was still at church. I needed this gut level praying before I prayed with my family or you. I had an inner core I needed for myself before I could pray for others. I know it was right to pray for others, but in my heart, I couldn't pray with faith until I had a restoration myself.

I hate fights. The fight was caused by my lack of quality prayer, Bible reading, ministering over the past three weeks. Working three jobs is a drain, and I wonder if the decision we made was our own decision or not. It seems to be a decision that drains spiritually in favor of getting more monetary support which are worldly motives. I pray that I'll understand the finality of the whole situation.

The beach is uncharacteristically calm. The sun warms my face, a rare event in our part of Oregon. Howard is sitting in the sand next to me. Nick is scooping up sand with a little shovel and burying Sara. Kyle is digging a hole to china with a clam shell.

"I feel that I eventually will be working two jobs instead of three." Howard continues a conversation he had started. "One of which will be the Columbia Press. I feel this job is what I want to do- a big break from Bio-products. I worked on my high school paper and loved it. It is an opening into a new trade and all the skills it involves- editing, writing, proofreading, correcting and reporting."

"You'd be good at that. You love to write. Would you quit Bio-products, then?"

"Yeah, I'm just not cut out to work in an industry."

"How about the preschool? You don't want to work there anymore either?" I ask.

"What about the handicap Thrift Store? You like working there, don't you?"

"Yeah, I do. I told you about the vision I had several weeks ago concerning this, didn't I? As I was praying, I had a flashback of the film we saw about St. Francis of Assisi, him standing on the wall of the church looking down at the physically handicapped people in the courtyard below. I feel that the Lord was indicating to me that this is where I should be. The church is supposed to care for these people. That job is *ministry!*" Howard says. "God will provide all our needs. That's a promise. So, whatever happens, if we seek His guidance daily, it will be all right because we'll be in His will."

I nod my head in agreement. "We'll get through this together," I say.

CHAPTER **10**

Howard's Journal

    I don't live to teach language arts fifteen minutes a day. I don't live to teach calendar ten minutes a day. I do live to instruct kids about Jesus. I do live to do the paper. I don't think I live to do anything! What do I live for? I was still in secular employment while Jan was living in the King's Service. I am ready to be in the King's service now, but where do I go? Ask the Lord where you shall serve, and He will show you.

    You can't have a divided vision. Marianne is a whole lot better at teaching kindergarten than I am.

    God has accepted the sacrifice of Abel, (Jan's) and refuted mine.

    I have no vision- all I know to do is the paper. It is my vision. The paper is my best form of service.

    The Lord has taken the last thing away from me. Where there is no vision, the people perish. I don't fit into staff meetings. I don't even know if I fit into the board- I don't know if I fit into your vision at all. The classroom could run very well without me even being there- I tried to stick myself to your vision. Vision- something you live for, eat, breathe, and would die for: in your sleep, one dreams about it. The Lord is my vision- but the same kind of 24-hour a day concentration is given to serving Him. You have that vision in the preschool whereas I don't.

    I want to give up all, but it's hard to give up all I'm familiar with. But we have to lay it all at the altar if we are to see God.

CHAPTER 11

"WHAT ARE YOU working on?" I ask Howard. He's sitting at his roll top desk. It's covered in piles of papers, his journal, his Bible, open to a page of scripture, a cup of pens standing in a corner and bills thrown into the envelope cubby. Howard's concertina sits on the top along with his open notebook of song chords. Keith Green is singing *There is a Redeemer* on the record player. I hear a tub of Legos being emptied out on the floor of Nick's bedroom. I'm hoping Nick will keep an eye on Kyle so that he doesn't put any in his mouth and choke on them. Sara sits at the table coloring with her markers neatly placed in their holder that Howard had made her for Christmas.

"I'm filling out an application to teach English in Japan," he says. "The application is due by the end of next week. They'll be having a job fair in Portland on January 16th. I thought you could call and get a hotel and we could spend Friday night and go to the job fair the next day. There are a lot of possibilities."

I did say that I was always one for adventures, right? I wasn't sure I was really ready to give up our life here, but I would hear his idea out and see which way the wind blew.

"Sounds good. I'll ask Marianne if she can watch the kids."

With temperatures in the low 40's, Howard and I zip up our coats and head to the Portland Convention center. We enter a room full of booths, each sporting piles of brochures and information. Some have fancy stand up posters proclaiming the benefits of working for them. Others are more mundane. There are jobs to teach in all sorts of countries- many in China and Japan, Taiwan, India, and Denmark. I'm not sure why Howard is drawn to Japan. Maybe that's what God's telling him.

We stop in front of a booth advertising jobs in Japan. Several people are there and speaking to the representative. Howard picks up a brochure. I listen in as the rep tells another couple about being provided an apartment, no, transportation is on your own, yes, the cost of living is higher than here, but their pay package and benefits make up for it. The couple takes the brochure and an application and walks away. Just as Howard and I move in to talk to the rep, he puts out a sign saying, Sorry, gone for the day, will return tomorrow.

Howard and I look at each other. We try to follow him, but he's instantly lost in the crowd.

Now what? We can only afford one night in a hotel and that was last night. This was the only booth for Japan.

"We could try another country," I suggest.

"No, I really feel like it was Japan we were supposed to go to," he says as we walk through the aisles to the door. He begins to bite his lip. We walk outside into the crisp air. We just stand there, immobilized. What to do now? Suddenly I see the representative catch the Max in front of us.

"Come on," I say and pull Howard to the Max to board. We get on two cars behind him, but we can see him through the windows. We go several stops into the heart of Portland. He gets out. We get out. We run to catch up with him, not sure what to say. We follow him as he goes up the steps of an older, brick apartment building. He's going to think we're creepers!

We watch him unlock his door and go in. We stand outside his door, out of breath and look at each other. Well? my eyes say. Howard knocks at the door. We wait a few seconds and hear footsteps. The representative opens the door.

"Yes?" he asks.

"Hello, um, well, we were just at your booth at the job fair and we really wanted to talk to you about teaching English in Japan," Howard says.

"I'd love to help you, but I really can't talk to you except at the fair. Come back tomorrow." He starts to shut the door.

"But we could only be here today," Howard pleads.

"I'm sorry," and he shuts the door.

We slowly back down the stairs and sit on the bottom steps. "Well, apparently I'm not hearing God clearly," Howard says. "Looks like this door is closed."

"Literally! There's always the commune," I say.

Back at home, Howard pulls out the brochure from Highway Missionary Society. There's no phone number, only an address. He sits down at his desk and writes a letter requesting that someone contact him. A week later we receive a phone call, someone calling from a pay phone. Howard sits at the kitchen table, twirling the phone cord around his finger. He nods, asks what living there is like on a daily basis. He continues to nod. Finally, he hands the phone over to me. She repeats what she has told Howard, about how you would be living in a common house, with a single large kitchen and outdoor outhouse. I nod, reliving my Takilma experience. She tells me about having a farm, raising their own sheep, pigs and cows for food. We have a large communal garden that everyone is expected to help with. She explains how everything is communal. You would be expected to give up everything you own and put it into the community for all to share. I'm repeating everything she says so that Howard can hear the conversation.

I nod, thinking of all my kids' toys, my sewing machine, my kitchen aid mixer. I'm not sure I'm ready to trust everyone with my things.

She continues telling me that you would be expected to give all income that you make into the commune. And also, any gifts that are given to you would go into the commune as well. Okay, now I'm picturing Lucie's monetary gifts to us and knowing she would go ballistic with this. At this point, I thank her for her call and hang up.

I sit down, look at Howard. He raises his eyebrows.

"Well?" he says.

"Well?" I say. "No. Just no! Maybe I'm just not a Book of Acts person. Maybe I'm just not trusting enough. But really, I can't see us living this lifestyle."

Howard nods. "I thought you'd say that."

"Are you disappointed?" I ask.

"Kinda," he says. "But we'll just get back on our knees and see what else God has for us."

Howard's Journal

All bridges going back have been burnt- not by me, but by God. Hard to have no safety valves, outlets- I assumed the main bridge was Japan's word, but it was right here at home- preschool closed to us, saying you have to move- that had been the outlet if all else failed, we could still have the preschool. I prayed that the Lord would shut the doors of three of the four opportunities we had. Within three days, two main doors were shut. I prayed wanting to do God's will, and He heard and answered. There comes a time when you can no longer live in the world and in the kingdom- you must choose one or the other. When the Lord shuts a door, nothing you can do can keep it open.

Do not worry about tomorrow, today has enough problems of its own.

CHAPTER **12**

Warrenton

"GREAT DINNER, JAN." Rudy wraps his arm around me and gives me a friendly peck on the cheek.

"Yeah, thanks for inviting us over! We hardly ever get out." Karen takes the cup of decaf I offer her in one hand and the decadent chocolate dessert in the other. We head to the living room.

"Tell us about your Asia plans, Colleen." It was so fun to have friends over. We hardly ever did. One, because we couldn't afford to make dinners for more than just us, and two, we just didn't seem to make the time.

I sit on the orange couch with my legs tucked under me. I turn on the lamp and reach for my quilt to work on.

"Well," she looks at Jerry, her husband of two years. "We'll be leaving this spring and study in Tokyo at the language immersion school. Then we'll be told our placement for mission work."

Jerry said, "We're a little nervous, because we're still not sure how God will provide for our finances. We've been able to raise two-thirds of it, but still have a way to go."

Rudy propped his hands behind his neck and stretched back on the couch. "God will come through. He always does if we stay in His will."

"Isn't that the truth," Howard said. He took a sip of his tea. "I mean, we're not rich, by any means, but we've got a roof over our heads and food in the cupboard!" He wipes the tea from his mustache with the back of his hand.

"Rich," says Rudy, "is not in physical things, it's in our relationship with the Lord."

"Hey, speaking of physical things, have you ever measured your legs?" Howard sets his cup on the coffee table. Everyone is looking quizzically at him. "No, I mean, have you ever seen if they're both the same length?"

Jerry says, "Yeah, I went to an evangelist once and he was claiming to heal people whose legs weren't the same length."

Howard gets down on the floor and stretches out. "Look at this," he says. "One leg isn't the same length as the other."

Rudy gets down on his knees and pulls on Howard's legs. Sure enough, his left leg is shorter. "Have you gone to a chiropractor?"

"Sure, I go once a week for my back. And my neck has a tweek in it. I need to ask him about this. I just realized it the other day after I got through jogging and was stretching. Know what else I noticed?"

We all look at him.

"What?" we say in unison. I roll my eyes. Not another ailment.

He grins. "No, this is serious. When I was dialing the phone the other day, I had a hard time putting my finger in the hole."

"Probably drunk!" I say, knowing that Howard never drinks anything but milk and water.

"Yeah, drunk in the spirit!" Rudy says. We all laugh.

"No, this is serious!" Howard continues, "I was trying to pour juice for Kyle and my hand started shaking when I held the pitcher. Something is going on."

I frown. "Is this all related to you falling at work the other day? Maybe you should ask the chiropractor," I say. Karen and Colleen nod agreement.

"There's one more thing... I was criticized for not keeping the drum beat last week at worship. Then when I really paid attention, I realized he was right. I noticed that I'm *not* always keeping the beat when I drum. Something is going on with me."

CHAPTER **13**

Portland, Oregon

APRIL FOOL'S DAY. What a joke! I shake my head. Unbelievable. I brush my hair away from my face and pull it into a pony and check myself in the rear-view mirror. I rub my shoulders- they're so tight. Who'd have ever thought we'd be going to Good Samaritan Hospital for tests, ever in our lifetime. We're too young for this. This happens to people in their seventies, not thirties.

Howard and I get out of the car. He holds my hand as we head to the front of the hospital. Birds are singing. Blue jays, I think. *Twitter chitter chitter.* Tulips interspersed with daffodils are in bloom along the sidewalk. Their happy bright yellow and red faces look up at me as if to say *life is beautiful.* I feel my heart pounding. My hands begin to feel clammy. I want to trust that everything will be ok but I'm entering into unfamiliar territory. A man in a suit and tie, swinging a briefcase walks by, whistling. He obviously isn't having tests done. Or going to see a loved one have tests done.

We enter through the building's revolving doors. I wonder if there must be another entrance for wheelchairs. I can just see someone in a wheelchair doing whoop-de-doos around the revolving doors. I chuckle. We walk to the receptionist desk immediately before us. The woman in a red floral dress directs us upstairs. We take the elevator- it's always more fun to push the buttons than to labor up the flight of stairs. I can see the kids running, racing to push the outside up and down buttons, fighting to get to push the number six button and again when we return. I think of them with Marianne. She is the best friend in the world. They'll be playing with Scott, Ike and McKenzie and having fun. Not a care in their sweet little heads. Not a clue that this could be a life changing experience.

The bell dings. The elevator stops with a lurch. We find Dr. Polaski's office. The receptionist smiles and hands Howard a clipboard with forms to fill out. We seat ourselves on the expensive upholstered chairs. Their blue weave reminds me of some my mother wove when I was a small girl. There is a stack of magazines- People, US News, Time, and Ladies Home Journal. I'm not really interested in movie star's wonderful or wretched lives. I glance at Howard as he fills out the forms. His left-hand jerks a bit as he holds the clipboard. He looks up-

"Insurance, hon. We have none."

I shrug. "Nice rhyme," I say. "God will make a way. He always does." I reach over and hold Howard's hand. I feel the softness and the hair on the back of his hand. He begins biting his lip again.

"Howard?" the nurse calls. He stands, begins to lose his balance but catches it. "Come this way," she says. Her scrubs- blue with bright green frogs jumping all over it. Happy frogs. Her brown hair swings to and fro as she bounces down the hall. I follow along. She shows him to a seat in the waiting room.

"Could you roll up your sleeve?" He does, dutifully. She places the stethoscope in her ears, wraps the band around his puny upper arms and starts pumping.

"139/67" she says as she replaces the equipment. Is that normal? I don't know. How often have I had my blood pressure taken? We're in our 30's!

"Stick this under your tongue," she says as she holds out the thermometer.

"Normal," she says.

She smiles cheerily and says, "The doctor will be with you in just a moment."

We look at each other and laugh. Isn't that what they always say and thirty minutes later they finally come in? There's a Van Gogh Sunflowers painting on the wall. I look out the window onto the tarred roof below. People are ambling down the street, seemingly without purpose. We hear a knock on the door.

We can't believe that he actually comes in right away. We look at each other and say "Wow" both at the same time. Howard puts his index finger and thumb together. I do the same and we give each other a little shake.

A stalky man, about six feet tall enters. He's wearing a gray tweed suit and dull, conservative, gray tie. He has on expensive gray pants, exquisitely pressed, and thin, matching gray socks. His wife must have dressed him. He must have a heck of a cleaning bill. He introduces himself.

"I'm Dr. Polaski." He shakes our hands firmly- like he thinks we're beginning a long-term relationship. His face is serious.

"So, tell me what's going on?"

Howard goes through the litany of things that have brought him here. His hand shaking, falling, losing his balance.

"I have a few tests to do before you have your CT scan. Please stand. Hold your hands to your sides parallel to the ground. Now touch your nose with your right hand. With your left hand. Both hands above your head."

I smile. Just like playing Simon Says. I notice the framed certificate on the wall. Harvard Medical School. He must know what he's doing. Isn't Harvard one of the best?

"Clap your hands." Dr. Polaski picks up a pencil with his long fingers and holds it in front of Howard's eyes. He moves it back and forth as Howard's eyes follow it. He moves it forward so that he crosses his eyes. He moves it towards his own nose and then in circles. He stops to write in his clipboard. *Clean, manicured fingernails.*

Dr. Polaski explains about the CT machine. "You'll be lying on a table that moves through a donut. As you are moved slowly by increments, x-rays will be taken of your brain. In all there will be nine pictures. You'll be able to see them as soon as you're through.

The nurse enters. "Come this way," she says. I look at Howard and whisper, "Is that all they know how to say?" He nods. She delivers us to a room with another attendant, this time a man. He's dressed in a white lab coat. Very slender, dark skin and deep brown eyes. Shiny black hair. He says hello in accented syllables and guides Howard to a table. I watch Howard lying on his back. He doesn't look relaxed to me. Is it because the table is metal and uncomfortable? Or is he just nervous. He's being slowly, mechanically, moved through an enormous donut. I wonder what it's like in there. Is it claustrophobic? Does it make noises? Does he feel like he's being zapped?

Howard's Journal

How can this be happening to me? I do not like this. I don't like doctors. They're all out to do their own thing and make their money. The technician looks at me with his cocoa eyes. "Are you comfortable?" he asks. How can I be comfortable, lying on a cold metal table, dressed in a thin hospital gown? Is this guy for real? I just look up at him and shake my head.

He places headphones on my ears. He asks what type of music I would like to listen to during the CT scan as it gets a little noisy. He explains how he's going to press a button and the table will move, with me on it, through a huge donut. I have thoughts of Star Trek. Maybe once I'm on the other side, I'll turn into another being. Better yet, slide through the donut, end up in heaven. Such a deal!

The machine starts to move. I close my eyes. I feel my body tense. I hear a banging sound. Muddy Waters pipes in. I start to tap my fingers on my sides. The table slides into the donut. My heart is pounding in my ears. Keep your mind on the music. Stay calm.

It's over before I know it. It's just an x-ray, I keep telling myself. Everything will be ok. God is not going to let anything happen to me that's not in his plan, right?

I WILL ENTER HIS GATES

Twenty minutes later we're seated back in the doc's office. He sits down, legs apart, elbows rested on his knees, hands clasped.

"I'm afraid I have some bad news." Howard and I look at each other. I reach for his hand. I entwine my fingers with his. We look up as the doctor pulls out the CT scan. It's like an x-ray, only divided into nine sections.

"This is your brain. What we see here is a spot on the left side of his brain. We are suspecting that it is a tumor."

We lean forward and see a white spot, small and round where he's pointing. He continues.

"It appears to be about the size of a walnut. It may be benign, but we need to go in to take a biopsy and find out. If we find it, we can remove it at the same time. We'd like you to come in next week and have this done. The surgeon is waiting to talk with you."

I'm stunned. My stomach does that loop-de-loop again. I'm not sure what to think. Brain surgery? Wait a minute. Like, cut into his brain?

The surgeon walks in.

"Good afternoon, Mr. and Mrs. Rea. I'm Dr. Stanzner." He holds out his hand to Howard.

"What will this surgery entail?" I ask. My thoughts are whizzing in my head. I feel my stomach do its wiggle thing. Come in next week? I've got a school to run. Benign? I've heard that word before, but doesn't it have something to do with cancer?

"How do you do it?" I blurt out.

His voice is grave. He looks at Howard. "First we have you come in for some blood work and tests. Then the day of surgery, we shave your head. We insert a dye through the artery in your groin. This goes into the brain so that when we are in there, we can distinguish the tumor. For a craniotomy, we cut from the top of your head to your ear, remove a piece of skull and take thin slices of the brain to determine where the tumor is. When it's done, I'll cover the opening in the skull with a piece of metal or fabric and then closes the incision."

I wince. I look at Howard. His knuckle is up biting his lip. His head is bent, shoulders rounded. His anxiety is contagious. How can it be that in one day your whole life can change its course? How is it that day after day you get up, take your shower, get the kids up, eat breakfast, go to work, come home, and the hum drum continues. And all of a sudden, a day comes that you realize that life will no longer be the same again?

"How long will I be in the hospital? I have to make a living," Howard says. I know he's trying to be brave.

"You should only be in for a few days. We'll get in there and remove the tumor and you should be on your way."

The doctor makes it sound as if it's no worse than having a broken arm. Well, if that's the case, what are we worried about? Doctors know what they're doing. Good Samaritan Hospital is supposed to be one of the best for brain surgery. Let's just get it over with and get on with life. Everything will be "all better" soon.

We schedule the surgery for the following week and head home.

"How'd the doctor visit go?" Mare asks as we pick up the kids. Sara does a head dive for my knees. I grab her hands and twirl her upside down. "OK. Just fine. Howard has to go in for brain surgery next week. Nothing to get excited about."

She narrows her eyes and looks at me. She puts the back of her hand on my forehead. "Are you feeling ok?" she asks. I smile, tentatively.

"They did a CT scan and found a walnut sized lump. They want to go in and take it out next week. They think they'll find it and then he can go home. And I don't need to be there while he recuperates- he'll be surrounded by care."

She looks at me skeptically.

"It'll be ok. Really." I snatch up the kids and head them out the door.

"You know I'll take the kids again for you." Marianne's voice follows us out to the car.

I WILL ENTER HIS GATES

"So, how did it go?" Dorothy asks, looking up from her books.

"Just dandy!" I say. "He's going in for surgery next week." I look at the calendar. "That would be Tuesday, April 12. I'll get Bonnie to cover for Howard's class. I'm sure you, the talented, capable secretary can keep the preschool in line while I'm gone." I look at her and smile pleadingly.

Dorothy rolls her eyes.

"How long do you think you will you be?"

"I expect a couple of days. They say they'll just go in, get the tumor out and it's gonna take a few days to recover and then he can come home."

She looks skeptically at me. "It'll be ok. Really," I say.

Surgery Day is here. The kids are safe and sound at Marianne's. Dorothy has preschool under control. Bonnie is taking Howard's class. We've packed his journal and pen and his Bible. He's all set.

"Here, put this on." The nurse holds out a blue hospital gown to Howard. He stretches it between his arms. "You want me to put this flimsy thing on?"

"You'll look debonair!" Rudy says. The nurse chuckles. Howard shakes his head. Rudy and Nancy Magathan have come for support.

We shut the door in the room. He undresses and puts on the gown. I tie the strings behind and give his skinny little buns a tweek. He jumps. Raises his eyebrows like, no one's in here, we're alone... I give him a light slap on the cheek.

"So now what do I do? Just lay around?" he asks.

"I suppose so." But, no time to waste here. A male nurse comes in. He's got two trays. One of needles, an IV connected to a bottle with blue stuff, a blood pressure cuff and more that I'm clueless about. Another has hair clippers. Howard raises his eyebrows. The nurse tells Howard to sit in a chair and begins to shave his head.

"You know what they say, bald men are sexy!" Rudy says. Howard's eyebrows raise as he looks at me. I wag my finger at him.

"They can shave my head, but they're not touching the beard!" he says.

"Maybe while the doctor's in there he could remove a few marbles," I say. I jump back just in time to avoid Howard swatting me on the arm.

The nurse takes Howard's blood pressure. 130/90. He puts some Betadine on a cotton ball and begins to rub it onto a spot on the upper inside thigh, near his crotch. He jumps. "That's cold! What are you doing?" Howard asks. He's not ready for this. Who would be? And for a guy that's super modest, this is really putting him over the edge.

"I'll be putting an IV in your artery that will carry blue dye into your brain. It will make the tumor stand out so that when they do the surgery, it will be evident, and they can remove it. Just relax."

"As I poke you with this nice little needle." I finish. I laugh. Howard is not laughing. He's starting to look tense. He raises his knuckle to his lip and bites.

There's a slight knock on the door. Another nurse joins us. Together, both nurses have Howard move onto a gurney. They wheel him out the door.

"Goodbye, world," he says and waves. Rudy and I watch them take him into the elevator. This can't really be happening. I thought I was going to be ok. I'm glad Rudy is there.

Nancy says, "There are worse things than dying." I look into her eyes. How can that possibly be? Tears begin to brim. She embraces me and lets me sob into her shoulder.

We sit on the waiting room couch. A woman wheels by, dressed in her blue hospital gown. Can't they choose another color, for pity sake? She has her head bent, looking at the floor. Her hands are clasping a hanky. The nurse rolls her back down the hall to her room.

I've looked at every magazine on the rack. Not really looked, turned pages. My stomach is about to burst. What is this feeling? My head is cloudy. I look at things and can't see them. My heart sounds like a train rumbling on the tracks.

"Let's go for a walk," Rudy says. I nod my head, but I don't really hear him talking to me. All I see is Howard, covered in a blue gown, lying in a surgery room, full of tubes and doctors hovering over him. They're cutting a line down his head and removing his skull. Removing his skull! Ugh. My heart is pounding its way through my ribs. It's so loud it's the only sound I hear. Pound. Pound. Pound. I can't do this. In a distant fog, I know Rudy is trying to talk to me. I don't hear him.

"Let's go for a walk," he says again, touching my elbow. I look at my watch. It's been two hours. He takes my elbow and leads me down the hall and through the doors. My head is bent as I watch the sidewalk. Careful not to step on a crack or I'll break my mother's back. Maybe that's what's happened here. Maybe I've fallen prey to some wives' tale, and this is what's become of it.

"Look! Here's Rosa's Restaurant. Famous for pastries! Let's get a piece of pie," Rudy says cheerfully. He guides me through the door. The hostess asks how many.

"Two," he says.

"Right this way," she says and leads us to a table. We pass the glass covered pastry shelf. Oodles of cinnamon rolls, puff pastries, pies and sweet rolls seek to grab our attention. The waitress leads us to a little booth in the back. I look around. The couple next to us are older, much older than I. They eat and just stare out in space. There's no conversation. Don't they appreciate each other? They both look healthy. Don't they see that they should be enjoying each moment they have together?

"What do you want to eat?" Rudy asks. He fingers the menu. Normally I would dive into a piece of Chocolate Velvet pie. I can't eat. I can't order. My stomach is turning, turning, turning. My head is just fog. My heart is thumping so loudly I can hear it. Surely, he can too. Surely the whole restaurant can hear it above the din of silverware clanking and conversations.

"Just coffee," I say. He orders a piece of rhubarb pie a la mode.

"Who did you say has the kids?" Rudy asks.

"Marianne."

"How's Nick doing in school?"

"Ok." I want to say more, but I just can't. I want to tell him Nick has to have a note home every day saying if he's on task or not. I want to tell him I'm worried that he won't succeed in school, won't even make it to fourth grade at this rate and that he doesn't have many friends. I want to tell him, but I can't.

"You know, you need to watch that Kyle. He's going to get himself killed running around with real screwdrivers and hammers! That kid's a nut!"

"Hibbers and scribers," I mumble. My voice is monotone. I don't want to talk. It takes all the energy I've got to respond. I know he's trying to get my mind off of things. But I don't want to talk. My stomach. I feel like I'm going to explode. God, please let Howard be all right. Please let him be all right.

I take a sip of my coffee. It's good. I hold the cup to my nose and let the steam and aroma flow. My hands are shaking. I put the cup back down. The scent of cinnamon and freshly baked rolls drifts to me. I wish I could eat. I look around at the other tables. How can everyone be so happy, or so full of everyday routine? Don't they know that my husband is being operated on right now? I watch the toddler in the highchair next to me as he keeps throwing his spoon on the floor. His mom picks it up and places it back onto the highchair, mid-sentence to her husband. He throws the spoon back down. Without a beat, she picks it back up again and places it on the tray. He throws it down again and giggles, looking at his mom. I want to pick the spoon up and throw it across the room so he can't do that anymore. Instead, I take another sip of coffee. I check my watch. Three hours.

"You know Jan," Rudy puts his hand on mine. "God is gonna take care of things. He always does. Romans 8:28- He causes all things to work together for good. I know it doesn't look that way now but trust Him. He knows what He's doing." I feel a hard lump rising in my throat. Tears slipped over the rims of my eyes and down my cheeks.

We walk the long corridor down the 8th floor. The tiles have recently been polished to a keen shine. I can almost see my reflection in them. Rudy leads me to a couch- black vinyl. I sit down momentarily. I stand back up and walk to the end of the hall and look out the window. It's starting to rain. Of course. I put my head on the cold glass and watch the raindrops as they roll down. One rolls straight down the window and then curves into a crooked path. Another comes down and when it gets there, swerves away. Just like my life, I think. Going straight as can be, and then, without warning, curves away.

Clump clump clump down those shiny tiles. I look up. It's Dr. Stanzner! Finally. I breathe a sigh of relief. I look anxiously at his face. He doesn't look relieved. Anything but. His face is serious, grave. Rudy is with him. I check my watch. It's been six hours. Six hours!

"Well?" I say anxiously.

"We couldn't find the tumor."

"Couldn't find the tumor?" I said. I don't believe him. Wait, he wouldn't be messing with me, would he?

"We got in there and couldn't find it. The procedure is to take a small slice and then give it to the pathologist who sits beside us with a microscope. He looks at it and tells us if that's the tumor. After fifteen slices, we closed Howard back up. The samples were inconclusive." Dr. Stanzner says.

"But I thought you said the dye would cause the tumor to stand out?" I feel my legs shaking. I lean against the wall to steady myself.

"A tumor can look exactly like the brain. It isn't that easy." He looks me in the eye, not unkindly. "What we did find is that it looks like lymphoma, a blood related cancer, that travels through the blood or spinal cord from the lymph glands but that is not usually found in the brain. And if it is, it's at the base of the neck, not on the side of the brain. However, if it were lymphoma, it would be very rare indeed."

"How can you take fifteen slices of your brain and not have it affect you?" I ask.

"They're very small. It shouldn't make a difference," he says.

Who prepares a person for this? I don't even know what to ask. No one prepared me for this test. No one said, ok, when you get to this point, you be sure and say blah blah blah. My legs feel weak, like I'm not going to be able to hold myself up. I try to stop my shaking hands. I feel the blood rushing to my face. I shake my head and put my clasped hands to my mouth, and I bite into my knuckles. Why was I stupid enough to believe in doctors?

"You may go in and see him shortly. I'll be by tomorrow to check on him and answer any more questions. Mrs. Rea, I'm sorry." He turns around and leaves.

Rudy and I walk into room 648. The one that would be his for the next three weeks. Howard is lying on the hospital bed, propped up. His head is wrapped in gauze. His eyes are closed, sleeping peacefully. I take the few steps closer to him. Rudy nudges his arm.

"Hey dude," Rudy says. Howard's eyes flutter open. "Hey there, Bud," he tries again. Howard gives a faint smile. "Hey, look who's here. Who's this beautiful woman?" he says as he nods at me. Howard slowly turned his head towards me.

"Mah wahfe," he says with a crooked smile. I'm not smiling. Rudy looks at me. Howard's words are slurred. I look at the nurse, puzzled. Had he had a stroke? My face is getting hot. I clench and unclench my hands. Anger lines my face. Why didn't the doctors tell us what was going to happen? Why hadn't they been more clear? Didn't they know we'd never experienced anything like this before and didn't know what to expect?

I take Howard's right hand. So limp. I look at the nurse again. "*What* is going on?" I ask.

"He's paralyzed on his right side," the nurse informs me.

"What?" I nearly shouted. Wait, what does this mean?

"You'll need to talk to the doctor tomorrow. They'll do some more tests and see the extent of it."

"Is this something that will stay? Will he always be paralyzed?" I asked incredulously. My mind is whirring. He won't be able to drive. If he can't talk again, he won't be able to work. No work, only my income. Three kids to raise. A wave of awareness is setting in, like when at the ocean and the huge waves curl up and over themselves. Only this time, I'm not watching it from the beach. I'm inside of it.

"I can't answer that. You'll have to ask Dr. Stanzner tomorrow," she replies. I can't believe this. No wonder Howard never trusted doctors!

We can see that he needs to rest, so we leave. It's a long drive home and I need to see the kids and relieve Marianne.

I drive the two hours to Good Sam the next day. The television is on. Grizzly Adams. Howard is watching it and tears begin to fall down into his beard. He raises his left hand and mimes playing his concertina.

"Never more," he says. I reach over and hug him. I feel a blooming of love for this man. I kiss his forehead. Get a grip, I think. I have to be strong. Now, who's in control of our life, I think. Is it not God, the Almighty, the powerful, living God? It is *not* the doctors, it is *not* our circumstances. Yes, I think, God will prevail. He is in all things. Yes, he works things to our good. And we *will* see his wonders.

A peace comes over me as I look at my husband. I feel the assurance that God is with us.

CHAPTER **14**

Portland

THERE'S A KNOCK on the door. Doctor Polaski enters Howard's hospital room.

"How are you doing today?" he asks.

Howard looks up at him.

"What's with the paralysis?" I ask.

"Something happened while in surgery. I can't really explain it. This isn't what usually happens." I watch as he takes out what looks like a wooden skewer. He pulls off Howard's rubber soled hospital socks. He begins to poke gently into the ball of his right foot. Howard doesn't move. He pokes it into the ball of his left foot. He jerks his foot. Dr. Polaski pokes the point into his right toes- first his big toe, then the rest. There is no movement.

Dr. Simonsen moves to the side of his bed and picks up Howard's right hand. He pokes his thumb, fingers and then the palm of his hand. No sign of his feeling anything.

"We'll get him started in physical therapy. He'll have to work on regaining his strength."

"Is he always going to be this way?" I ask.

"It's hard to say. He may regain a lot with the therapy. Let's just keep a watch on him and see." He walks out of the room.

I want to believe things are going to be ok. I have to be strong. Surely this is going to be a test of our faith. Why do we proclaim to be

I WILL ENTER HIS GATES

Christians, if we don't live it? If we don't believe it?

Howard tries to lift his hand and motions to me. I hold onto his hands and look into his blue eyes. "Baahck door," he says. Back door? What is he talking about?

"Baahck door," he repeats. "Sara."

My mind is racing. What is he trying to tell me? I want him to just spit it out, but he can't. He can't say more than a word or two. I can tell he's exhausted.

"Howard, tell me more. Was it at our house?" He nods emphatically. Why did this have such meaning to him?

"Keys," he says. Ok! Yes! I've got it!

"When you found the keys with Sara in the back window, right? God must have been showing you a sign." He nods as his is eyes well up with tears.

Life in the hospital becomes routine. We begin to know the names and shifts of all the nurses. We expect the doctor to come in for less than five minutes a day. Blood pressures are taken, IV's are adjusted, and catheter bags are emptied. He is soon able to support himself using a walker. The speech therapist works with him to regain sentences and the occupational therapist tries to get him to put square blocks into square holes.

I begin driving back and forth from Warrenton to Portland daily, a two hour drive each way. I fill the time with prayer for everyone I know, including the doctors that I don't trust. I sing every praise song I can recall, immersing myself with psalms and promises. So now is why I've memorized scripture. I think I'm starting to get it.

Romans 8:28 All things work together for good.

Psalm 56:8 He holds all your tears in a bottle.

Joshua 1:9 Have I not commanded you? Be strong and courageous. Do not be frightened, and do not be dismayed, for the Lord your God is with you wherever you go.

Proverbs 3:5,6 Trust in the Lord with all your heart and lean not on your own understanding; in all your ways acknowledge him and he will make your paths straight.

II Corinthians 1:3,4 Praise be to the God and Father of our Lord Jesus Christ, the Father of compassion and the God of all comfort, Who comforts us in all our troubles, so that we can comfort those in any trouble with the comfort we ourselves receive.

The doctors have still not positively diagnosed Howard's condition. All the pathology reports were negative for cancer. Even though they think that it is a tumor, they can't proceed with any treatment. Chemotherapy, radiation and cobalt treatments are out of the questions without a positive diagnosis. They begin medication treatments of Decadron, a drug to reduce the swelling caused by the mass in his brain, and Phenobarbitol to prevent seizures, as we discover that any brain surgery begins the possibilities of these.

I go to book stores and look for anything I can find on the brain. I can't afford to buy the books, so I sit and read, drinking in every drop of information.

```
Glioblastoma, anaplastic astrocytoma is ma-
lignant and grows and spreads aggressively
accounting for more than 50% of tumors. It
is an accumulation of a mass of tissue formed
by abnormal cells. No one knows what causes
tumors. Tumor cells grow even though your
body doesn't need them and unlike normal old
cells, they don't die. They grow as more and
more cells are added to the mass.
    Benign brain tumors usually have clearly
defined borders and usually are not deep-
ly rooted in brain tissues. This makes them
```

easier to remove.

Brain tumors damage the cells around them by causing inflammation and putting increased pressure on the tissue under and around it as well as inside the skull.

And

A requirement for a diagnosis of aphasia is that, prior to the illness or injury, the person's language skills were normal. The difficulties of people with aphasia can range from occasional trouble finding words to losing the ability to speak, read, or write, but does not affect intelligence. Nonaffluent aphasias is speech that is very halting and effortful and may consist of just one or two words at a time.

Yes, that's him. I spend long hours trying to help Howard find words. He describes, with much difficulty, his word retrieval like the mark on the wheel in the electric meter box. The wheel turns slowly, and you only get to see the mark once per minute. That mark is his word he's trying to retrieve, and he has one opportunity to blurt it out until it surfaces again.

Word by painful word, through many tears, he asks question after question. Will he ever be the same again? Will I continue to love him, or will I leave him? Will he be institutionalized? Can he ever work again? Will he die and have to leave his children behind, unable to see them grow up? My heart is broken, but I try to calm his fears and give him hope. But really? He can't even feed himself, go to the toilet alone or shower. I continually mask my own doubts and fears.

"Where God?" he asks.

I grab my Bible which is sitting on the night stand beside him. I open to I Corinthians 13:12 "For now we see only puzzling reflections in a mirror, now I know in part, but then I shall know fully."

Howard's Journal

There come (sic) a time when I go home. When? What them (sic). One day at a time, I know. But, in terms of practical consideration, a consideration of time. For the time being, (6 months). Are you going to sacrifice your time to me? A year perhaps. Two years perhaps. That what it may take to get on my feet again. Are you willing to make the sacrifice? I may not be normal again at all. I may die two or three years down years (sic) the road. But, in term (sic) of a completely different lifestyle, are you ready now. And, that's what it would be, a completely different lifestyle. Are you willing to sacrifice two or three years of your existence for me? That's what would boiled(sic) down to. Two or three years of normalcy now to die in two or three years. Or in the case of Zacherian (Zacharias) fourteen months of muteness to get all back again at the end of that time, and to carry as normal again as normal (sic).

What crueler thing to happen in the prime of life than than (sic) normalcy in the prime of life. Confine of home far more appealing than confines of hospital, though unless you can stay with me.

Idiocity- I can't get words right for the life of me. I doubt I'll ever be normal again. (in terms of thought pattern). Way my mind is working right now, I am so frustrated. Bright spots, but few and far between. Three or four weeks but six month almost defeat me. And, then, Ive (sic) got the cat skan to contend with with (sic) after I get stronger. And then I get thought all a shuffle.

Four hours- this much.

It hurts me to hear doctors talk about normal things, when I doing those things no later than two week ago today!

And the people came to see what had happened. And they came to Jesus and observed the man who had been demon possessed sitting down, clothed and in his right mind. I feel that something came out during the seizure (maybe even legion) and since then, I've been in my right mind.

The nurse comes in. She has a half dozen cards in her hands.

"Here's your mail for today! Man alive, you have got a lot of friends!" she says. She points to the wall where we've wallpapered it with cards and pictures. A couple of Mylar balloons bounce in the corner. There begins to be something different about this hospital room. There's a presence in our midst.

"Hey Howard," I say, reminded by the mail. "I've got something special for you today!" Howard looks up at me. He raises his eyebrows.

"It's a tape that our brothers and sisters at Philadelphia Church have made. It has messages to you from everyone." I take out a cassette player from my tote bag and plug it in. I push play.

"This is Marnie, your roving reporter here at Philadelphia Church and we're here to say hello to you and from time to time have someone stop by to give you a word of encouragement."

"Hi Howard, this is Sven. I hope you're feeling much better."

"This is Shary. We're at church for a potluck entertaining a pastoral candidate. I've kept up with Colleen and Jerry on how you're doing. I'm keeping you in my prayers. I love you."

"Hi, this is Sandra. I'm gonna tell you one of my favorite jokes. There were three men stranded on an island. One was from Norway, one was Swedish, and one was a Dane. There was a genie in a bottle, and he was going to give them each one wish. (Can you tell my preschool story telling is wearing off?) Anyway, the first man said he really wanted to return to Norway. And poof, he was back. The second one said, I'd really like to return to Sweden to see my family and poof, he was back. The third one said, I'm lonely. I wish I had my friends back."

Howard gives a crooked smile.

"Howard, this is Bob. I've been lifting up prayers. If you believe in God as strong as I know you do, you'll be pulling through. Praise you Jesus, Amen."

"In the background you can hear the people milling about and the youth choir is practicing. Hang in there," Marnie says.

"Hi, this is Jared. "He sounds embarrassed. "I miss you and hope you get well soon." He's only twelve, so I imagine this is intimidating.

"Hello, this is Valerie. We miss you!"

"Hello Howard, this is Howard. We have to keep thinking good thoughts. Proverbs 3:4,5 we are to trust the Lord with all our hearts and not lean to our own understanding. And that lean should be underlined, asterisked and the whole ball of wax because of what's going on and if we're looking at what we're seeing we're all in serious troubles. So, don't lean- God bless you brother, we love you."

"This is Dick- I was up to see you today, but you were up having a CT scan. I hope everything works out ok. I hope that calendar I got for you will keep track of things for you. I'll see you on June 4. The Lord be with you and keep you in Jesus name."

I am amazed at how many friends we have!

"This is Chuck. Sorry you're up there, hope you're getting over what you've got. We're praying for you. Get back down here amongst your brothers and your sisters."

"This is Dick speaking. We're offering up prayers every hour. We wish you real good luck there. We keep you in mind all the time."

"Hey, that's Grampa Knotts!" Sara exclaims. I nod. He's not really their Grampa, but we've kind of adopted him and his wife since our own families are so far away.

"Hi Howard, my name's Tera, I'm seven. I'm praying for you."
Her voice is so sweet and trusting.

"Howard, this is Larry. Just want you to know we're praying for you. Cathy and I both. God bless you, we're behind you all the way."

I WILL ENTER HIS GATES

"Hi Jan and Howard, this is Janet. Just want to say I'm praying for you and love you. We miss you on the worship team and can't wait for you to get back to drumming."

"Hi Howard and Jan, this is Gene and Peggy. Praying for you."

"Dennis- we hope to see you soon."

Another nurse stops by and lingers. She doesn't want to leave.

Hi Howard, this is Terri and Tom and we want you to know we're praying for you and are going to fast for you too."

"Hi," a little voice. "That was Rachel who's two."

"This is John and Eleanor. We're praying for you. It's good we have a God who is for us."

"We're the Bobsey twins- Bob and Deanna. I'm looking forward to the next preschool bazaar so get your little buns back here and get working on that thing."

"This is Linda. Hi, I know that with our prayers that the Lord is going to sustain you and get you through these things. And I know Jan, with you standing by to give him strength, that's the best thing you can do for him. I know the times Chuck and I went through when he was in the hospital but with the prayers of everyone it helped us through. And Howard, Chuck still has the model railroad you gave him and if you get better you can come over and spend some time with him."

"We're remembering you in our prayers every day. Marie"

I look over at Howard. They're still coming. His eyes are tearing up.

"This is Peggy. Hi, we sure love you. I have a scripture for you. *They that wait upon the Lord will mount up on wings as eagles.* And you're going to be walking and running. Lord bless you. We love you."

Howard raises his arm as if in flight. He looks up as if to heaven.

"Delores and Ray, we're all praying for you. Hang in there cuz God is on the throne. Bless you both. You too Jan."

"Bill. Hang in there boy. Keep 'em cooking. You hang in there too Jan, Bless you both".

"This is Sam. Sue and I and the girls are really praying for you, and Jan and the children. We know you really want to get out of there soon."

"Hello, this is John, some of us have to be pulled veritably from the brink of the fire."

Marnie chimes in. "Our evening of entertainment and song is beginning. Maybe you can sing along with us."

The music begins. Sara, Nick and I begin to sing with them. Howard picks up every few words.

> *I've got a river of life flowing out of me*
> *Makes the lame to walk and the blind to see*
> *Opens prison doors sets the captives free.*
> *I've got a river of life flowing out of me.*
> *Spring up O well, within my soul*
> *Spring up O well and make me whole*
> *Spring up O well and bring to me*
> *That life abundantly.*

I hold Howard's hand. We both feel such strength and hope in knowing that if nothing else, God is hearing the prayers of his people. And He will answer in His own way. Maybe a full healing, maybe a spiritual healing. Either way, we have asked to be in His will and be used by Him.

Howard's Journal

I feel that the Lord is hand-feeding me tidbits of meat (insights), but I can't handle a full load yet. He wants me to concentrate on my own relationship with Him right now. Before, I tried to ingest too much too fast and wound up bloated- a lot of head knowledge but no heart knowledge.

I have been ordained by God to have a brain tumor. Once I gave my life to Christ, I told him that he was in control. In the hospital, I dedicated my life to being a slave to Christ- whatever He wants, I will do, I have no rights if I am a true disciple. "A slave is not above his master."

CHAPTER **15**

Portland

Psalm 15:1
O Lord, who may abide in thy tent? Who may dwell on the Holy hill? He who walks with integrity, and works righteousness, and speaks truth in his heart. He who does these things will never be shaken.

April 30
Howard's fingers moved! It was just a little twitch, but they moved! In the midst of a desert, even a drop of water can mean life. Hope. The essence of things hoped for- the conviction of things not yet seen. Maybe he was going to recover.

We both look up as the physical therapist knocks at the doorway.

"Hi, my name's Jeff." He extends his hand. Howard lamely lifts his right hand to shake and then shakes his head in defeat.

"No problem," Jeff says.

"Let's see how you're doing, young man."

He removes the covers and prods Howard's legs with a probe. It's week two and still no feeling in his right leg. He helps Howard sit up and slides his legs over the edge of the bed.

"Today we're going to see how well you can walk down the hall."

Howard looks at him skeptically.

I WILL ENTER HIS GATES

"We'll use a walker. Just one step at a time. That's how it's done!" he says.

He maneuvers the walker in front of Howard. I go to the back of the bed and tighten the strings on the back of his hospital gown. Then I throw a robe over his shoulders. Jeff helps him get his useless right arm through the sleeve and ties the belt. I slip on some hospital footie socks, the ones with the gripper bottoms.

"Ok, count of three let's see if we can get you up. Place your left hand on the handle. Slide your feet down to the floor. That's it. I'll support your right hand on the frame."

Howard scrunches his face as he concentrates on each direction he's been given. Every aspect of life has become a challenge. All we want him to do is stand up for now and it takes almost all he's got in him to do that.

His feet planted on the ground, Jeff reaches around Howard's waist and pulls him forward. He moves out of the way and places his hand on the handle. He attaches a Velcro strap to hold his hand in place.

"Okey dokey! Looks like we're ready for a stroll."

Howard's glasses have slipped down his nose. I push them back up for him.

First you have to push the walker, then take a step. Jeff explains to me that as well as relearning how to walk, he will have to exercise his hip muscles since they will be out of whack with a different gait.

As much as I would love to watch this new lesson, I have to get back to the kids. I kiss Howard on the forehead, squeeze his hand and head for my car. When I return the next day, I find this written on a piece of notebook paper, sitting on the stand.

Howard's Journal
April 12-May 7
What I learned in the hospital
My life is not my own from the time I commit my life to Christ. He

can use it as He sees fit. I am a slave to Christ.

Death is the mere beginning of life. Eternal Life! If we really believe it, we will rejoice in death.

I never doubted that Christ was the son of God, but I got a new understanding of the awe He struck into people while He was here on earth. People marveled; they had never seen anything like that before. Nor had I, until I went into the hospital.

Cease from striving and then the Lord will work. Striving indicates we are trying to do it ourselves.

We are going to stand before God on judgement day, not the church board. We are answerable to Him and Him only for the life we lead. The church board had determined not to back the paper, so I quit putting it out. But we are unmovable to God to get His word out.

He is there. Even though you can't see him, he wants you know that He is there. Before I prayed out of obedience to the Word because it said to. But He is there, and He wants us to know He is there, and can ask him to do things and they will be done, because we are his adopted children and He loves us completely.

CHAPTER **16**

Warrenton

"WHEN ARE WE going to get there?" Nick asks. All three kids sit in the back seat of the Nissan station wagon.

"We're almost to the hospital now," I say. After twenty-five days, they're releasing Howard. I'm so relieved that I won't have to travel back and forth every day. Maybe we can put together some semblance of a normal life again.

I park the car in the parking garage. The kids pile out.

"Don't run!" I say. Sara grabs Kyle's hand. I lead them through the revolving doors of the hospital. They fight about who is going to push the buttons in the elevator, just as I predicted.

"Push six," I say. The doors open, and we traipse down the familiar hall to Howard's room. He looks up from the soft green lounge chair and puts on his biggest smile. One side of his mouth is still slack.

"Daddy!" they chorus and run to him.

"Careful," I say. "Not too rough!"

"Where Sara?" he asks. I look around. Where is she? I go out in the hall and she's flat against the wall next to the door.

"Come on in," I coax. She shakes her head. "It's ok. It's your daddy. Come see him." She peeks her head around the corner and tentatively looks in. Then returns to her safe spot. I take her hand and lead her in. She hides behind my legs.

"Sara," Howard says. He holds out his hands to her.

She looks at his limp hands and cowers into my legs.

I look around the room. What needs to be done before he can be discharged? "Sara, help me pull the cards off the wall", I say. I ball up the sticky tack to save for later. The balloons are limp, so I ask Nick to pop them and throw them away, a job that he relishes.

I find Howard's shoes and slide them onto his feet. His right foot is a challenge because it's limp and unresponsive. Howard points to the bedside table where his recently crafted orthotic is. The therapists have ordered a special plastic foot brace to keep his foot from dropping. I grab it and put it on. I slip his foot into the new Velcro shoes I bought for him. Tying shoes won't be something he'll ever do again.

Soon the nurse comes with the discharge papers to sign. I'm going to miss this nurse. She has been a strength to us. She explains to him about his prescriptions.

"The Dilantin, given to stop seizures, should be taken four times a day. Common side effects of Dilantin include headache, nausea, vomiting, constipation, dizziness, drowsiness, slurred speech, loss of balance or coordination, swollen or tender gums, insomnia, nervousness, tremors, or rash." Howard and I look at each other. The nurse proceeds to tell us about the Phenobarbital. It is for the short-term treatment of sleeplessness, the relief of anxiety, tension, and fear, and the treatment of certain types of seizures. A follow-up visit with Dr. Stanzner is made for two weeks from now.

I hand Sara the overnight bag with all of Howard's things in it, a small wash basin, shampoo, and lotions, a water bottle with Good Samaritan Hospital printed on the side, his Bible and journal.

Nick holds onto Howard's good elbow to help support him while he holds his cane in his right hand. He lifts his foot by lifting his hip. His paralyzed, atrophied right arm and hand are bent and stiff at his side. He holds his cane with his left hand. Kyle runs ahead to the elevator to be the first to push the down button.

Once in the car, I remind Howard that today is Nick's ninth birthday and we're going to celebrate at Chuck E. Cheese's. I had wracked my brain to think of something that would be fun and special for

Nick. Usually we just had a special friend over.

I pull into the parking lot and park in a handicapped spot. Wow. I've never had to use one of those before. This is going to be convenient. The kids jump out, slamming the doors behind them and run to the entrance. I walk around to the other side of the car and help Howard out.

We get inside where Nick is tugging me to the counter.

"Pepperoni," he says. "I want pepperoni!"

I order and tell the waitress that it's his ninth birthday. She smiles and congratulates him. She hands him five shiny gold tokens and tells him he can choose whichever games he wants to play. I purchase more coins for Sara and Kyle. I seat Howard at a table to wait. Music and pings and dings sound from the various games. Lights are flashing reds, yellow, greens. I follow the excited kids to the pinball and various game machines. We are entranced when a waiter taps me on the shoulder.

"Ma'am," he says. "Is that your car parked in the handicapped space?"

"Yes," I say, turning from the game to look at him.

"You have to move your car. You don't have a handicap tag," he says.

"I know, but I just got my husband from the hospital from having brain surgery," I say, dumbfounded.

"I'm sorry ma'am, but that's the rules. You have to have a tag or you can't park there."

"Are you serious?" I ask, bewildered.

"Do I need to get the manager?" he asks.

"No, I'll go move my car, I guess," I say.

I'm not sure what to do. I don't want to drag the kids away from their game, and yet it's not a place I feel comfortable leaving them in without supervision. You can't really call Howard supervision. I finally decide to make a run for it and hope they'll be ok.

I return and the pizza is ready. I call the kids over to the table and open the box. Tantalizing smells emit. Howard breathes them in.

"Real food," he says as he reaches for a piece. The cheese starts to drip and he tries to catch it with his other hand. His fingers are unresponsive.

Sara looks at him and slides down into her seat.

"What's wrong with your hand, daddy?" Nick asks.

Tears start to form in Howard's eyes.

The traffic is light as we travel back home. Howard is amazed at how green everything is. Things have changed since he went into the hospital a month ago.

He points to some flowers.

"Look, the blooms are flowering," he says. I look at him.

"Daddy," Sara says, "That's not right, you silly! The flowers are blooming." He gives her a weak smile.

We pull into our driveway. I take a deep breath. We've been so sheltered the past month. I'm not sure how this is going to play out, Howard being home.

"Mom, look at our house! It's painted red!" Sara exclaims.

"Wow! And look at that," Nick says, pointing. "Someone built a ramp to the front door." It was true. Someone had been anticipating our return home. Friends. True friends think of what we will need in advance and make it happen. We later find out that it was Ray Cameron and Dick Ford, friends from church who built the ramp. And Rudy and the Bible Study group who painted.

I get Howard into the house and situated on the couch. He looks around at everything as if each little detail is new. He's exhausted. Kyle is toddling through the house, made-up noises filling the air. Nick chases after him, telling him to stop. Sara pulls out some paper and scissors to create something, singing all the while. Howard puts his hands on either side of his head and yells "Stop!" I tell the Nick to go outside and play and then I help Howard into the bedroom to rest. I shake my head. This is going to be tougher than I thought.

Mounds of laundry are piled up. I haven't cleaned the house in a month. It's starting to look like a haunted house with cobwebs hanging from the ceiling. Open cracker boxes, miscellaneous plates and cups and a peanut butter jar sit on the counter from when I would dash in, get a bite and rush back out again the few minutes I was home between hospital visits. I start to pick up. Piles of bills and mail clutter the counter. I'll get to that later.

My mind is whirring with all the things I have to catch up on. Megan, one of my preschool teachers, has quit. I have to advertise and get someone to replace her. I'm sure other things are falling apart there as well since I haven't been able to devote my time to it. Thank goodness for Dorothy.

I guess I better think of something for dinner. I open the cupboard door. There's not much there. I'm going to have to go to the grocery store and restock. But wait, can I leave Howard alone? I go in to check on him. He's still asleep. I grab my checkbook, load up the kids and head quickly to Sentry Market. Ten miles seems like a lifetime. Ok, what do I need? Milk, eggs, cheese, hamburger, noodles. I try to think of everything before I get there so I can make a dash for it. What if something happens to him while I'm gone? What if he falls out of bed and can't get up? Or has to go to the bathroom but slips and falls. He could break his hip. There's nothing to him, he's so frail. Toothpaste. We're out of toothpaste.

When I return home, Howard is sitting at his desk, writing in his journal. I breathe a sigh of relief.

Howard's Journal
May 5, 1983

I was cut down so that I would still be able to inherit the kingdom of God, although as through fire.

The lame and the cripples are strong people. They have to be, with all the mental anxiety they go through. They have to have a fighting spirit to go through life missing a hand or a foot and still be strong through it all.

My sign is my limp and lifeless right arm. Just as Cain was given a mark because he had sinned, so too my mark indicated my sin. I am marked to show what happens to one who habitually sins against the Lord- that he can enter heaven, but only via much tribulation. Even so, God loved Cain.

Howard looks up from his writing. His glasses are falling down his nose.

"You're home! Where did you go?" he asks.

"I left you a note," I say. "You must not have seen it. I had to get groceries. You got out of bed ok?"

He nods.

"Do you think you could help me take a shower? No more sponge baths!" he says.

OK, what's this going to look like?

"Sure," I say. "Let me get the groceries put away first."

When I finish, he's already in the bathroom. He's trying to take off his t-shirt, but with only one hand, it's difficult. I pull it over his head and slide down his sweat pants. I run the water. We look at the tub and then at each other. How is he going to get in? If we had only known the future, we could have taken out the tub and put in a shower with a low lip.

I'm going to need to get someone to put in a bar for him to grab on to. We both realize that this is not going to happen for him today- this I'm-going-to-take-a-shower-and-feel-normal-again. What if I get him into the shower and he falls? I'm not strong enough to lift him back up. I grab a washcloth and some soap and hand it to him to suds down.

"Mom," Sara calls. "Kyle is stinky!" She's drug him into the bathroom by the arm, holding her nose.

After I get Kyle's diaper changed, I head to the kitchen to start spaghetti. No, not spaghetti. How will Howard eat that? You have to cut it or slurp it. Hamburger then. No, that takes two hands. I finally decide on stir fry with rice.

"Jan," Howard calls. "Come help me get dressed."

I finish up the dinner dishes. Howard is sitting at the table still, talking on the phone to Rudy, the cord wrapped around the fingers of his left hand. His speech is better, but not yet perfect.

"Time for a bath," I call out to Sara. "Go get Kyle, too."

I run the water, grateful that I can just turn hot water on at the tap. I remember living in that little cabin on Elder Creek outside of Takilma. So grateful for running water that I didn't have to pipe in and a hot water heater. And a toilet that I could use *in* the house. One that flushed. Although, the beauty of it was that you could look at the river while you did your business.

Kyle and Sara splash in the tub. I soap up Sara's hair and make doggie ears. Kyle laughs. I pour water over it and wash away the soap.

Wrapped in hooded towels, they run towards the living room. Suddenly I hear a thud. I run to the kitchen towards the sound. There in front of me is Howard, lying on the floor twitching. His eyes are rolling, and his hand is twitching violently. I don't know what to do.

Howard's Journal

All the time I was having the seizure, I was consciously aware of my thoughts, but I was in a state of blackout.

When I first was going into the seizure, I was putting on my pj's and had them half on. When I looked at Jan, she looked far off, then got blurry, then contorted.

I remember my arm uncontrollably buckling. At this time, I blacked out, but I was aware of Jan talking to me as I lie down on the floor. All the time I was in a state of blackout.

I remembered thinking, don't swallow your tongue, and wondering what would happen if I did swallow it. I knew it would be worse. I could see myself squirming uncontrollably all over the room as in an epileptic fit. As it was, I just lay on the floor in one spot and, I am told by Jan, shook uncontrollably. All this time I was in a state of blackout.

I could feel it was subsiding, but it took an inordinate amount of time, I thought, to go away. The whole seizure took one or so minutes.

I remember Jan coming back from the kitchen with the pills. I knew where she had gone and knew what she was doing. She put one pill in my mouth and said, drink this. I did and got a very little water into my mouth but got the pill down.

I took two more pills (Dilantin), I had one in my mouth and told her to wait before giving me the water. Don't go too fast, I said. After a while, I took it. Then one more, I took this last one when I was fully recovered.

Afterwards, immediately, my right leg was very hot, and my right arm at first had no control. I couldn't bend my right leg. But after about three or four minutes, I could bend the leg and could move my arm around into all the positions.

After a night's rest, I am back to where I was before the seizure. I walk with a little bit of stiffness in my right leg.

CHAPTER **17**

Warrenton

Howard's Journal
June 15, 1983

Malachi 3:9
 Bring the full tithe into the storehouse.

 We are under obligation to bring the full tithe into the storehouse- if we miss two months, we are obligated to make restitution to the Lord.

Mark 12:41-44
 For they put in out of their surplus, but she, out of her poverty.

 She put in all she owned all she had to live on. We will just treat it like one of the worldly bills, paying off $20 at a time, erasing the sum until it has all been erased from our obligation to the Lord.

JULY 9
 How do we rebuke the devourer? Bills are destroying us as I sit here. A new obligation to the world- debt of society, arrives almost daily to our house, friendly reminders of our earthly, worldly existence.

I feel like I have created this mess. During my wavering years, I didn't tithe, or else tithed begrudgingly. Now, it's all coming back on us as a family. Things were going along just fine until May when I had my first experience (weak of revelations) with the Lord. Since October 17 when I feel I was ushered into a whole new dimension, things have really gotten out of hand. May-Jan. Bank loan, Pacific Power, October- cancel car insurance, a bill daily and all the money is gone. Again I ask- how does one rebuke the devourer?

Bring the whole tithe into the storehouse. Then I will rebuke the devourer.

Obey- We have to show good faith and reliance upon his word, and then he will hear from heaven.

Pray for forgiveness for not tithing.

Don't look at anything other than the Lord and keep your eyes on the Lord and his provision through this whole financial difficulty. If you take your eyes off the Lord, you will see the turmoil of the seas crashing all round. Like Peter walking on the water. Seeing the wind, he became afraid, and beginning to sink, he cried out, Lord save me! Keep your eyes, heart, soul, mind and strength focused upon the Lord continually, If you look anywhere else, you lose your focus and you will become off balanced.

Concerning Tithing- I was making God into my own image. I was taking a principle and turning it completely around to suit my desires. it boils down to my selfishness. I wasn't going to give to a church when the church wasn't meeting my needs. But it was God's proclamation to tithe, to give to the servants of God. "The thresher ought to thresh in hope of sharing the crops." A proclamation may be taken lightly, but a proclamation is still a proclamation, and the proclaimer will deal with those according to how they obeyed or explained away.

Why do we so often doubt that God will be true to His Word? He continually says that He will meet our needs, and yet before Howard went into the hospital, I would grit my teeth as I tithed, anxious that we would have need of that amount. I write out a measly check and place it in the basket. Before church is over, a man approaches and places a $20 bill in Howard's shirt pocket. Two others randomly give us checks equaling ten times the amount I had tithed- more than Howard's normal pay check.

"I'm on my last Dilantin pill. And I only have four Phenobarbytol left, and my Decadron will be empty soon as well," Howard says, holding a bottle in his left hand.

"Not sure what we should do," I say, knowing that if he goes off the pills, there's going to be hell to pay. The Dilantin keeps him from having seizures. The Pheno is also an anti-convulsant. We don't have any insurance. The Pheno is only $10 for 100 pills. We could probably swing that. The Decadron is $20 and another $12 for the Dilantin. I know it might not seem like a lot of money to some people, but right now, every penny counts.

"Maybe we could ask the church if they could pay for them for this month and we'll see what happens next month."

"I don't really want to do that," he replies.

"I know, honey, but what other choice do we have?" I ask. I think, we could just not tithe this month. Wouldn't it be the same thing? Then I think of Ananias and Saphira. Don't really want to go down that road.

We haven't received any bills yet from the hospital. It's got to be way into the $100,000's by now. Not anything we'll be able to pay in our lifetime. Thinking I should probably find out, I pick up the business card from Good Sam and dial the number.

"Good Samaritan Hospital, this is Cheryl."

"Hi Cheryl, could you please connect me to the finance department."

"One moment please."

"Finance Department, this is Eileen. How may I help you?"

"I'm calling because my husband, Howard Rea, had brain surgery a month ago in your hospital and we haven't received a bill yet."

"Ok, let me check on that." Beethoven's Fifth is playing in the background. After what seems like forever, Eileen comes back on.

"Tell me your husband's name and birthdate. I'm just not finding anything in the records yet."

"Robert Howard Rea III, December 21, 1946."

"Ok, I'll look through the files again." Finally, she returns.

"Mrs. Rea, I see that he had surgery, but there isn't a bill."

"What do you mean there isn't a bill?"

"There isn't going to be a bill. The doctors wrote it off." I'm flabbergasted.

"But what about the hospital? He was in intensive care and in the hospital for three weeks."

"There's no bill for the hospital either. You are one lucky family!" she says.

I hang up the phone and just sit there, awestruck.

I've closed the preschool for the summer so that everyone can have a break. That also means that I'm not working. We have applied for disability benefits, but it is a long, slow process.

I look in the cupboards, trying to decide what to make for dinner tonight. We're down to one can of beans. One. Well Ok then. Beans it is.

Howard and I walk into the County Building and find the office for Food Stamps benefits. I open the door for Howard who trails along behind, carefully lifting his left foot so he doesn't trip. He holds the door open with his elbow since he can't grasp with his curled hand. We find the room and sit down in a small office. A woman with a clipboard begins to ask us questions.

"How many in the household?"

"Five."

"How much monthly income do you have?

"None over the summer."

"Does anyone have a disability?"

"Yes."

"Are you receiving Social Security or other income?"

"No."

"Do you own your house?"

"Yes, we're making payments for $135 per month."

"Do you own your car?"

"Yes, it's paid off."

"Oh. That's not good. I'm sorry, but we can't give benefits if you own a vehicle."

I look at Howard and my jaw drops.

"What?" I ask, trying not to shout. "We don't have any income. If I don't have a car I can't possibly get to work. It's the only real asset we have and we need it."

She looks over her glasses at me and says, "There is one option. You could sell your car to someone for $1 and then you wouldn't own it. You would have to hand over the Title to them," she says.

We ask if we can discuss this alone. She nods and leaves.

"What should we do?" I ask Howard.

"I don't think it would be right to sell the car to anyone. They are asking us to be deceitful and that would not be in line with scripture," he says.

"Just another opportunity to trust in how God will provide for us," I say. We get up and walk out of the building.

When we arrive home, I help Howard undo his seatbelt and open the car door for him. He lifts his limp leg with his hands, using his right forearm and hoists it out the door. I hand him his cane and he walks carefully up the ramp. There on the front porch are four bags of groceries. I laugh and look at him. I unlock the door and carry the bags inside. I unpack tuna, mayonnaise, two loaves of bread, salad veggies, peanut butter, and cheese. We haven't seen so much food in over a month. At the bottom, I find a note-

The Lord told us to buy some groceries for you. We hope you and your kids are ok with what we chose. Don't give up hope in the Lord.

We love you! Dr. and Mrs. Leinesar

AUGUST 3

Beginning with Monday night, August 1, the following have happened to us.

Nancy and Dick brought by a freezer full of elk meat (about 20 or 40 pieces) and two bags of groceries.

Jan was given $20 by Judy and was told to take the three loaves of bread (fresh bread at that!) at the church office.

We went by the Human Resources Office to get food stamps and got $300 worth. We had been given only $150 before.

On Tuesday Aug 2, Martha and Ray phoned up and said that a donation of $500 had been given to the preschool and $200 dollars had been given for our use.

We returned to Good Sam Hospital to pay bills and found that the hospital had no record of my stay there.

We went to the zoo and got in for free because Tuesday was no-pay day at the zoo.

Jan's mom gave us $500.

FEBRUARY 6

I have been cut off from having any earthly desires- I have been set apart for God's work- the things of this world (money) are meaningless to me- I hate them, I shun them- I am of the attitude that I just want to go home and let someone else worry about the problems of the world- In the world you will have tribulation. Constant harassment from all sides, unceasing, unending for as far as the eyes can see, problem after problem after problem with no end in sight- indeed, with no end period- eternity spent in frustration, anxiety, worry- hell that is what it is going to be like. Might as well throw in all the gray areas with two right answers- choose your own- you can have it any way you want it, - try to maintain the proper balance between drill on the one hand and freedom on the other. Add to that the constant friendly reminders that bill hasn't been paid, and on and on and on. That's why I say that I just want to go home and let someone else *worry about the problems- they are just not worth it all- if I didn't have the kids and Jan, I would seriously consider a Saint Francis of Assisi lifestyle- I wouldn't trade it, but that's the way I would choose to change if it everything was taken away from me, including the family. It is amazing how much tension one can absorb- I myself have short-circuited, I went on high extension for 36 years and I have just burnt out. I'm sorry, Jan, but I am just burnt out- I have very little emotional drive left in me. I am spent. That's why I feel that I am useless to the world. I hate the world and all its fickle earthly systems. Yet, I must stay in the world to do battle until the Lord calls me home. This is the sacrifice I must make; to stay in the world, when I would much rather leave it.*

APRIL 17

A moral God but not personal, I found to know not only personal, but the Son of God! Luke warmness in my soul has subsided. Sell all and go even to the outer limit of the world, even to Hammond. But lifestyle that the rub. Sold out for Jesus. Even if I have to get up at two o'clock to pray I will for Jesus sake. I will sacrifice, all for Jesus sake.

And they were amazed, and they all glorified God, and were filled with fear.

For there went virtue out of him and he healed them all.

Blessed are ye that weep now; for ye shall laugh

One day at a time- your life may be required of you at any time
Get serious with God.

Parable of the sower. Before the hospitalization, I was operating in the third position in the parable- choked with worry, In the hospital, I made the subtle transfer, to the #4 position- learning fruit with perseverance.

Love is not having anything against anyone, not ever for a righteous cause. Love is the standard of Christianity and 1 Corinthians defines that quality of love.

NOVEMBER 18

Doubts unsubstantiated are lies. Listening to doubts is the same thing as listening to Satan- that's the same thing he did- he spoke doubts.

Faith is trusting in the reality of what you can't see, not trusting in the reality of doubts.

Faith is trusting in God, not trusting in the doubts about my condition.

Trusting in God is standing on the rock of what you know is there, not standing on the sand of wavering doubt. Sand will wash away, rock won't.

Howard's first drum set

Howard's high school group

Howard loved playing concertina

Before the brain tumor

Making memories

Aunt Betty and Nick

Wedding dress sewn on the treadle machine

Howard and Jan's wedding 1975

Pregnant with Kyle

Jan with preschool students

The guinea pig present was under this tree

After surgery with his cane

Jan's friend Marianne

Howard's friend Rudy

The last photo of Howard

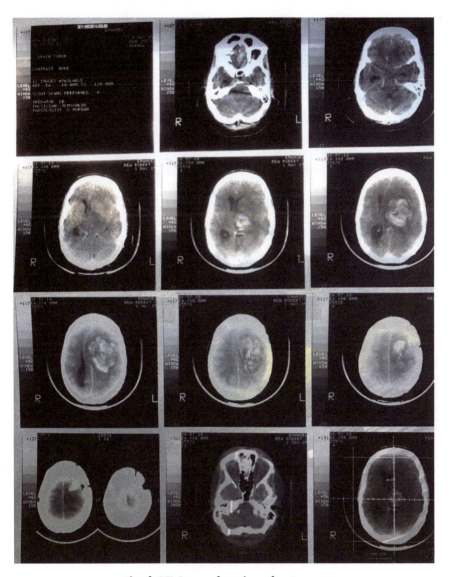

Final CT Scan showing the tumor

Gravestone Eternal Valley Memorial Park, Newhall, California

CHAPTER 18

Our friend Sandi shared that she believed God had a special few that He showed how Christ had suffered. They are indeed privileged, if what I believe to be the principle of opposites is true. In this world, you must give to get in the kingdom; in this world, the first shall be last in the kingdom. If we hold up a positive picture, the complete opposite is true in the kingdom- a perfect negative. So, one would feel I have been given the privilege of suffering in this world. Without suffering, there would be none of the thoughts- and those are precious. I have always told the Lord that I wanted to experience what he meant when he said what He said, experience the pureness of His gospel. I think He is letting me do that, and it hurts. It hurt Him, and it hurts me, He cried, and I cry.

John 2:17
  Zeal for thy house will consume me.

I am not going to offer a compromise platter to the Lord. I need for my decisions to be based on what the Lord has said. I won't do what my conscience won't allow me to do. I need for my decisions to be based on what the Lord has said in His word, rather than on the wisdom of man. Because, what man has said may seem to be logical, but what the Word says may contradict. I cannot waver from any decisions I make, because wavering allows doubt to enter, and doubt has been my downfall. I must seek my answers from the Lord, and I must not be dissuaded by what man says. Most men doubt the Word, and so when counsel is not based on it, men waver.

I have to stick by what the Bible says in spite of what I am feeling; I should bring what I am feeling in accordance with what the Bible says, rather than allow doubt.

John 2:4
My hour has not yet come.
John 2:13-16
My temple is beset by all sorts of doubt and fears.

Is the spot getting bigger? Will it leave me like a vegetable? What would have happened if I hadn't had the surgery? Will my fingers and leg come back? Doubts, fears, worries. Cast them out of the temple! The same things that were making the temple an impure place resides within us. The father's house ought to be a temple standing firm on the Word of God, but the moneychangers had made it into a place where the things of God were ignored- a den of thieves. We must be reaffirming God's Word in our prayer lives, rather than having it turned into a den of darkness, doubts and fears.

February 6
I am suffering the shame of being entrapped in this body- potbellied and back and chest as well as limp right side, broken out unmercifully, humiliated, from which there is no release from this body until death.

Romans 7:24
Wretched man that I am! Who will set me free from the body of this death? Thanks be to God through Jesus Christ our Lord.

I wonder if God had set me apart to be a eunuch for God (Paul's term) means unmarried- but I chose the other alternative of marriage. But I am just as good as a eunuch now. I have always wanted to devote myself to God. That was the choice I found myself making nine years ago when I chose to get married, rather than choosing the alternative. I believe that God is now telling me- via circumstances- to separate myself to Him and for his purposes in the way Jesus and Paul says.

1 Corinth 7: 32, 35
I want you to be free from anxieties. The unmarried man is anxious about the things of the Lord, how to please the Lord. But the married man is anxious about worldly things, how to please his wife, and his interests are divided. And the unmarried or betrothed woman is anxious about the things of the Lord, how to be holy in body and spirit. I say this to promote good order and to secure your undivided devotion to the Lord.

CHAPTER 19

Portland

1 Corinthians 1:27
God has chosen the weak things of the world to shame the wise and the weak things of this world to shame those that are strong.

Physically, I am a shambles- right leg practically useless, right arm useless, gut bulging (ever-expanding) and medication induced acne covering my chest and back.
This He has chosen to shame the wise that no man boasts before the Lord.

"HOW DID THE follow up go?" Marianne asks.

"Not that great. Dr. Stanzner wants Howard to go to Oregon Health Sciences University for a needle biopsy. You can only imagine how that went over."

She shakes her head. "Do you need me to watch the kids again for you?"

I nod. Again. There for me again.

"When's his appointment?" she asks.

"In two weeks. It's like asking him to put his hand on a hot stove again. He's not taking this well."

"Guess it's time to entreat the Lord again," she says. "His unfailing love will come through."

I know it's true, but sometimes, it just feels like it's never going to end. What is it about learning to trust? When you become a Christian, you are asked to learn to trust. But how does that actually come about? I search through the recesses of my mind to people in my life that I have trusted. And how did it turn out in the end? Like my French teacher. Or my dad who abandoned us. Or my mother-in-law Lucie who is always critical of everything we do and say. I guess I could say I trust my own mother. She has for sure set boundaries when I was pregnant with Nick. But didn't she come through with a random check for $500 to help us out and call with words of encouragement and advice? I definitely trust Marianne. She has given unfailing love.

"How do you trust God?" I ask. "The Bible says, I think in the book of Proverbs to 'Trust in the Lord with all your heart and lean not on your own understanding.' I mean, how do you really know that the promises He has in the Bible are true?"

"Life lessons," she says. "You know how in the Old Testament God told the people to set up stones along the way so that those who passed by would be reminded of what God had done for them. That's what we need to do in some fashion. We need to remember all the times that God has been there or kept His promises to us so that we can learn to rely on His faithfulness."

"Like what stones would you erect?" I ask.

Like when Isaac fell out of the back of the pickup. I was driving 45 mph, getting ready to approach the Hwy 101. I screamed "Jesus" as I came to a panicked stop. I leapt out running to pick him up. He ran to me crying,

"Mommy, why did you throw me out of the truck?" He was completely unharmed.

Or like the time we were learning to budget my husband Steve's once a month teacher's pay check and about three weeks into it we were out of money. I had a houseful of kids- eight or nine, I can't remember if we'd adopted the last four yet. We were driving home from Astoria, over the bridge and praying,

"Lord, I have nothing in the house to feed the kids for lunch. Please send something our way between here and home."

We arrived home and the kids scrambled out while I got Isaac out of his car seat. As I passed through the kitchen, the phone rang. It was Shary.

"Marianne, I know this might sound crazy, but I just got home from the surplus store. I have a five-pound brick of cheese. I was asking God who might need this, and your name passed into my head. Any chance you could use this?"

"Could I ever!" I answered back. I was just asking God to supply a lunch for these hungry kids of mine. Can I run by now and pick it up?

"Better yet, I'll deliver it," she said.

As I hung up the phone, I glanced out the side yard and noticed that my neighbor's apple tree had dropped a dozen or more juicy apples on our side of the fence.

"Kids," I called out, "Let's go gather the apples from the side yard and slice them up. We're having apples and cheese for lunch."

"Ok, so like when we took off and moved to Warrenton and God landed us at Philadelphia Church where I started my dream job of a preschool," I say.

"Or, like when all your hospital bills were wiped away," Marianne says. "Philippians 4:19. My God will supply every need according to his riches in glory."

Finding a parking space at Oregon Health Science University Hospital is a daunting task. Even though I know how to get to Good Sam now and maneuver through Portland traffic, taking the right turn off and bridges to OHSU is more than nerve wracking. Howard holds the map and watches road signs while I drive, trying to avoid fast moving locals and massive freight trucks. It doesn't help that the windshield wipers are going furiously, and water is spraying onto the car obscuring our vision. How do you spell S T R E S S!

After winding ourselves up Terwilliger Blvd we finally find the parking garage. Our appointment is at ten o'clock and it was 9:45 now. I guess everyone has an appointment at ten because we have to circle up several levels to find a spot.

"What building is it in? Which floor?" I ask.

"Just give me a minute, will you?" Howard snaps as he opens the door, turns sideways, lifts his left leg out with his hands, adjusts his foot, reaches for his cane, steadies himself and shuts the door. He hands me the paper with the information on it.

I look up at the old bricks and ancient windows. We proceed through a narrow hallway to the entrance where I hand the receptionist the page. She directs us to the correct floor and room. I look at Howard as we walk slowly down the hall. His beard had become scraggly because he refused to cut it, deciding it was one thing he could control in his life. He needs a haircut. That's my fault. I've been too busy holding down the fort to attend to his needs. Who was going to see him anyways? He rarely goes out except to church now.

Dr. Shin talks with us briefly, reviewing Howard's inability to always get sentences correct, his limping, the boils on his chest from the medications, the seizures, the extended stomach, also from the medications. Dr. Shin wants Dr. Brown to do another CT scan and orders a needle biopsy. This time he is hoping to find the tumor and again, try to determine if it is malignant or not. Howard's knuckle goes to his lip, his paralyzed arm tenses up and becomes stiff. His brows are knit. I can't blame him for being stressed. How would I be if they wanted to fool with my brain after how the surgery had left me the last time?

After Howard had been admitted to the hospital, given a gown. Why does he have to wear a gown until they actually take him in which isn't until tomorrow? I look around the room. There are six beds. It doesn't occur to me that this is because we don't have insurance. That if we did, we could have a private room. There's a young man in the bed across from Howard. His mother and wife are there with him. He looks like a wreck. He makes Howard look like a magazine model. This man can barely put together a sentence. His eyes are vacant. I imagine he would have a lot of trouble walking as well. His wife makes eye contact with me and comes over to visit.

"Hi, my name is Maria." She holds out her hand. I shake hers. "I assume your husband has a brain tumor?"

"Yes, I say, and yours?"

"Yes, we've been here for three weeks now. They are trying to decide if there is anything else they can do for him."

"What was he like before this?" I didn't want to ask, but it just blurted out.

"He was just a normal guy. He had a job as an engineer. We have two kids. He was a great dad." I try to look like I'm having a normal conversation with a normal person. But I feel like I just ate a whole loaf of artisan bread. I tense up as my mind whirs to the reality that this could be my husband. That this probably was going to be my husband.

"How did you know he had the tumor?" I ask.

"He started getting headaches that wouldn't go away. And then he would be disoriented. People at work started to notice things. This was two years ago."

I fill her in on our story.

"Let me know if I can help you in any way," she says as she walks back to her husband's bed. "It's not an easy road to follow."

Howard is in the surgery room having the biopsy. They say they are going to insert a long needle, guided by the CT scan, into where they think the tumor is and try to extract a piece of it to give to the pathologist. If that's not it, they will try again until they find it. My mind is wondering how the results are going to possibly be any better than when they cut into him before. What other debilitating effects am I going to have to deal with when he gets out of this? I let out a long sigh.

The results come back. They are not what we expected. They found . . . nothing.

"How can you find nothing?" I ask, my voice almost a scream. "How can you be guided by the CT scan and find nothing? Are you telling me that he had to go through this twice and still you can't find it? Is there even really anything in there? What the heck?" I feel my blood pressure rising. I'm not willing to be calm any more. This is getting to be abuse.

Dr. Shin waits for me to finish my rant. Howard is lying in the bed with a small bandage covering the spot where they went in. His eyes move between me and Dr. Shin.

"We are not exactly sure. We see the tumor on the CT scan. But when we took multiple samples, it came back as normal. We are thinking it's possible that there are multiple tumors and that the needle is avoiding them, going between them, and not giving us the results, we need. I'm sorry that I can't give you more than that," he says.

"Isn't there anything you can do?" I ask, hoping that for by some amazing miracle, the doctor could be our salvation.

"We could try chemotherapy to try to shrink the tumor, but since we don't really know if it's cancer, I wouldn't advise it. There are a lot of side effects."

"Like what?" I ask.

"Like vomiting, weight loss, hair loss, weakness, loss of appetite."

"No!" Howard says. His no is firm, but any speaking is difficult for him. I'm instantly transported back to Good Sam where he had aphasia. But then I know that this is because he's stressed, not anything more.

"So, what do we anticipate is going to happen? What will be the progression?" I ask. My shoulders have slumped.

"It will likely grow until it's too big for his brain," he says.

"Then what? How will he die?" I ask. I want to know everything. I want to know what to expect.

"Well, patients generally either die from choking and suffocating because they forget how to swallow, or hemorrhaging- the blood vessels burst."

Tears are glistening in Howard's long eyelashes. "I don't want to suffocate or choke."

I take his hand and look into his eyes. What else can I do. Nothing looks good at this point.

CHAPTER **20**

Astoria, Oregon

October 13, 1983

Mert Miller
Attorney of Law
Astoria, Oregon

Dear Mr. Miller,
We thought it might be wise to write and tell you our concerns and history rather than spending time in your office reviewing all of this.
In February 1982, Howard had an injury while working at Bioproducts in Hammond, which caused him to limp on his right leg. In February 1983, he noticed that he was losing coordination in his right arm. He was drumming and unable to keep the beat as before and had to concentrate to dial the phone because his finger was unsteady. Dr. Andresson, the chiropractor, recommended that Howard see a neurologist in July of '82 because he thought that it was a problem with the neurosystem that caused him to limp. In March, '83 Howard finally saw Dr. Polaski, the neurologist from Good Samaritan Hospital in Portland who comes to Columbia Memorial once a month.
Dr. Polaski scheduled Howard for a CT scan April 1. The CT scan showed a spot on the left side of the brain. At this point, Dr. Polaski

felt that the arm weakness was progressive from the leg and felt sure that Howard had a tumor. He consulted with the surgeon, Dr. Polaski and he concurred that Howard should have surgery a soon as possible. April 12 was scheduled for hospital entrance and April 14 he had surgery.

We were told that they would do a biopsy, and hopefully find the tumor and remove it. They told us recovery time would be a week to two weeks. They did not tell us of any possible side effects or anything that we might expect to have happen. The surgery took six hours. They took fifteen biopsy samples and closed him up finding no conclusive evidence that there was a tumor. Dr. Polaski said that the surrounding cells looked like lymphoma- a cancer that travels through the blood or spinal cord from the lymph glands. Normally it doesn't go into the brain, and if it does, it would settle at the top of the spinal cord.

If it were indeed lymphoma located on the front left side of his brain, it would be very rare indeed.

Following surgery, Howard lost his ability to speak and was completely paralyzed on his right side. He was in the hospital for twenty-five days. When he left, he was just beginning to walk, his speech was nearly regained, but he had a hard time with reasoning and thinking skills. Now, he still confuses words, limps when he walks, worse than before the surgery and has limited use of his right arm. He is still unable to button his clothes and put on contacts and hammer a nail. He drops anything in his right hand, cannot dig with a shovel or tie his shoe laces. He loses his balance continually which causes him to fall. A wheelbarrow tips over when he uses it. When teaching, he can't hold a book and point to the pictures, and has trouble putting the needle on the record player. He loses food off his fork when he eats and can't carry two cups of coffee at the same time, to name a few examples. All this is a result of the paralysis.

Because he had a minor seizure in the hospital after the surgery (he had never had one before surgery) he is now on Dilantin medication. The side effects we've noticed are extreme mood changes, unclear thinking and long-term effects are a rotting of the gums. We are believing from the doctors that he will have to be on this drug for the rest of his life.

Dr. Polaski told us that he did not expect any of this to happen to Howard. We had no insurance and were concerned about paying for all of this. While in the hospital, Dr. Polaski had been taking Howard's case to Dr. Shin at the University Hospital, he being one of the head neurologists there. He recommended before we left the hospital that we go see him at a later date. Dr. Polaski called us at home the next week and said she had scheduled an appointment with Dr. Shin for May 20. We went to see him, they did another CT scan-which he said was fuzzy but didn't see any noticeable growth of the "tumor". (They were still convinced that it was a tumor). We complained about having to pay for a poor x-ray and he said he'd take care of it. He strongly encouraged us to check into the University hospital to have a needle biopsy done, a technique that was new to the medical field. We were quite hesitant to have this done, but in the end, they convinced us that this was necessary. We asked about the possible side effects, knowing that the doctor wasn't going to tell us otherwise. He replied that there might be bleeding. I asked what could be caused from the bleeding. He replied that it would cause a stroke. If he had a stroke, it would be 100% paralyzation. He said it all very matter-of-factly and rushed on to say that of course, it was our decision and it wasn't any skin off his back if we didn't do it. He talked very quickly, and Howard kept trying to get a word in edgewise.

He finally told the doctor to shut up, so he could talk. Howard told him that he felt like they were experimenting on him and that he wanted time to consider it. Then Dr. Shin left. This conversation took about ten minutes. About ten minutes later, Dr. Brown came in and spent two hours trying to convince us to do it. We finally consented, partly because they instilled a fear in us that it could only get worse; and partly because she said she herself was going to do the biopsy. We were not consenting to having Dr. Shin.

Howard went in from 1:00-2:00 pm to have the needle biopsy. They took the liberty of doing it twice. His stay in the hospital was for two days. His bill amounted to $52,300 discounted to $600 from the hospital. His bill from Dr. Shin was $1800. The radiologist charged $220.

We called Dr. Shin's office the day they said they would have the results, and the secretary would not tell us the results. He had an appointment here with Dr. Polaski that Friday, June 24th. We told him we couldn't get the results and he called immediately and got them. They were "inconclusive of a tumor" Dr. Shin had sent the biopsy off to different parts of the country hoping to find one doctor to agree that it was lymphoma. He was so convinced that's what it was. He had even been pushing chemotherapy before they knew it to be true!

The reason for the June 24 appointment with Dr. Polaski was because of Howard's total setback due to anxiety of returning to the hospital.

Since that time, we've been concentrating on our future existence. We applied for welfare at the advice of University Hospital to have medical bills paid. We would have qualified except for owning our Datsun putting us $1200 over. We were advised by friends to sign over the title for $1 to a friend, but we felt like that was deceptive and not right for a Christian to do.

Howard has been able, until two weeks ago, to receive unemployment benefits. He has applied for Social Security disability. He was sent to their neurologist in Portland for an exam. After explaining the situation, beginning from the leg limping due to BioProducts, he said he didn't understand how they could say the weak arm was progressive from the leg. We said that we had been saying that all along. He also said that Howard had been given such a high-powered battery of tests at Good Sam that they hadn't found anything, they weren't likely to. He said that in his opinion, a needle biopsy was worthless.

As it stands now, Social Security benefits have not arrived yet. Howard can't work and still receive them. We felt it would be better for him to be a volunteer teacher at the preschool rather than be paid since it might be that he couldn't continue because of his disability, and once he's lost his disability status, he can't regain it.

If he were to apply out in the "real world" chances are slim that he would get a decent job. He's only working half days now as it is.

When all is said and done, we are concerned about a lifetime disability that he has to live with along with the surrounding implications, when had he not gone into surgery to begin with, the doctors would have very little less knowledge than they do now. They were inconclusive that it was tumor in early June- they still are inconclusive today.

Our questions are:

1) Do we have a right, or grounds to sue, just to enable us to live (get by) for the rest of Howard's life

2) Is this an ethical thing to consider, being a Christian

3) How would this affect the doctors?

4) Are there possible alternatives and

5) Is this your area of expertise?

We are not out to defame Dr. Polaski or any of these doctors. We fear not being able to survive and feel a great unfairness in the situation.

Your thoughts on the matter would be greatly appreciated, any questions and concerns can read us at 861-3458.

Jan and Howard Rea

We're sitting in the comfortable arm chairs in the office of Mert Miller. His hands are folded, index fingers touching and pointing upwards.

"I've read your letter. You two have experienced quite a lot in the past year," he says.

We nod. Waiting. Is this something we even want to pursue? Several well-meaning friends have encouraged us to go this route, so here we are.

"There are several things we need to look at. One is Standard of Care. Doctors are human. But they are expected to be competent. An expert would be needed to testify to the standard. Two, we would have to prove that the doctor breached that standard of care. Did the doctor fail to do something a competent doctor would have done?"

Certainly, there's been a breach. How could Howard end up paralyzed from this surgery? It was supposed to be a simple operation. Go in, remove the tumor, close him up.

"Three," Mert continues, "is causation. We have to prove the doctor's breach caused the injury you're concerned about. For example, if a doctor did surgery without using gloves and you ended up paralyzed, the breach of not wearing gloves is not what caused the paralyzation. If you had ended up with a serious infection because of it, that would be a valid breach."

We both nod.

"Four, damages. What types of injuries did you suffer due to the surgery? What medical costs has this incurred? How is this preventing you from earning a living? What are all of the other costs that have added up and what will be the financial burden not only now, but in the future because of this? A monetary amount will help with care and lost income."

I look at Howard. His knuckle is bent and pushing against his lower lip as he bites the skin. I'm starting to see dollar signs, money going down the tubes. There are so many bills, and so much that I have to do to care for him. What about the kids? How will I afford to raise them? What Howard is getting from disability isn't a whole heck of a lot.

"Five, we have to look at what we call acceptable risk. By definition this is risk for which the benefits rank larger than the potential hazards.

Many doctors are conscientious and want to do what's right. If they've made a mistake, they might have cause to be held accountable. Is medical malpractice a viable option? There are acceptable risks for that surgical procedure. The bad thing that happened doesn't necessarily mean he could have avoided it.

In the case of brain surgery, possible risks associated include:

allergic reaction to anesthesia
bleeding in the brain

a blood clot
brain swelling
coma
impaired speech, vision, coordination, or balance
infection in the brain or at the wound site
memory problems
seizures
stroke

Howard pushes his glasses up. I know he wishes he could still wear his contacts because his glasses always slip down. But I tried putting them in for him. It ranked just below giving him a suppository.

Howard replies. "My brain is swelling, according to the last CT scans. I have impaired speech, vision, coordination and balance. I have memory problems and I have seizures. And I assume all of this was because of a possible stroke. So then, no, we can't say this was necessarily negligence."

"I can pursue this if you want," Mert says. "You need to know that it will take some time. It would need to go to an appeal court and proceed through litigation. The doctor would not lose his license."

I'm seeing dollar signs again, but this time not ones that will go in my pocket. "How much would it cost?" I ask.

"This consult is free. I would keep track of my hours and if you were awarded a settlement, my fees would be taken from that."

"And if not?" Howard asks.

Richard's eyes hold Howard's steadily. "If not, then you would have to pay the bill."

Howard steadies his left hand on his cane and starts to stand up. I grab his elbow and steady him.

"I guess this isn't a path we'll walk down," Howard says, and we head to the door. "Or should I say limp down."

Howard's Journal

Jesus walked out of a crowd who were going to stone Him for it was not yet time for His death. If I am going to sue, the one I would be suing would be God, not the doctors. I am not happy with what you have done, and I am going to get satisfaction. What God did was to give me a much closer relationship with Him than I ever had. Through the turmoil of this tumor, He has answered my prayer that I would be closer to Him and has imparted a Spirit of release on me.

CHAPTER **21**

Warrenton

Psalm 9:11 Sing praises to the Lord who dwells in Zion. Declare among the people His deeds. He does not forget the cry of the afflicted.

"JAN, I HAVE the articles ready for you to type," Howard says, looking up from his desk. He pushes his glasses up from his nose.

Howard has created a small Christian newspaper, *The Times, Heralding His Return*. The local small-town newspaper, The Columbia Press, had taken him under their wing and was publishing for a small price. The papers were distributed in local stores, churches and public areas.

He pulls up a chair beside my small desk. I roll a piece of paper into my IBM Selectric. I am so grateful to have a typewriter with the x key. I can correct mistakes as I go. And believe me, I make quite a few mistakes. Howard begins to read what he has carefully written on his yellow steno pad.

I begin typing:

The Times is a newspaper designed for outreach and discipleship to residents of Clatsop County. It is produced on a non-profit basis by a group of independent Christians to create a sense of unity and love between denominations within the Body of Christ and to draw non-believers into the reality of knowing Jesus. All monetary "profit" will be put into the production of the next issue of The Times. No denomination or group of sponsors is represented by, The Times.

The production staff of the Times is composed of Christian men and women who are in good standing in their own churches, and who produce the paper within a sense of God's call to them.

The Times is not affiliated with any missionary, evangelical, charitable, or denominational group or society.

The staff of this newspaper believes that God is Triune, made of the Persons of the Father, Son, and Holy Spirit. We believe that Jesus Christ is God Incarnate, Son of the Father, who was born of a virgin, walked the earth and worked miracles, preached God's true word to mankind, was crucified, died on the cross, and was physically resurrected in a supreme act of atonement for the sins of mankind. We believe in water baptism, the empowering and indwelling of the Holy Spirit in the lives of all Christians, the resurrection of the body and life eternal for the redeemed in God's Kingdom. We believe that the gifts of the Spirit are in operation today, and that miracles still occur today as a result of God's direct intervention into human history.

I stop. Wouldn't it be nice if there were some way to save the initial paragraphs, so I didn't have to retype them each issue? "So, what articles do you have ready for this issue?" I ask.

"Here's what I have so far. I think this should equal about twelve pages: "Sodom and Gomorrah, Wiped out in Worst Disaster Since Flood" *(written as if current news),"* Homosexual Ruling, Clatsop Court Cases moving Faster", " On Abortion- Standing Up For What We Believe", " Lifestyle" *(an article on Dr. Larry Goza)* and "Censors Interpret Nude Scenes" *(The CBS decision of censorship based on "Gauguin the Savage").*

"Ok, "I say. "Better get started before the kids find a reason to interrupt us."

Devastation in Path of St. Helens
...after all the facts of the Mt. St Helens eruption, the ripping apart of the peak dropping the elevation from 9.677 to 8. 400 feet, the heated mudslides, the "fried" people, the five to ten million cubic yards of silt and debris into the Cowlitz River, the fifteen to twenty tons of ash per acre fallen on crops, and the explosion which seared a fifteen mile wide arc around the mountain's north flank.

And yet, we are all- each and every one of us- within the danger zone. For, when disaster strikes, most of us are either thinking "it could never happen to me", or, we are trying to show that, because we can explain, then we are in control.

But man is not in control, and such catastrophes will happen again. Volcanoes and tornadoes and hurricanes are created by terms which man can not alter. They are sent, not by mother nature, but by our Lord God, to cause us to re-examine our self- sufficiency, our pride, our haughtiness, and our self-exaltation, not only as a nation, but also as individuals. We exalt ourselves against the Lord when we tell ourselves that we don't need Him.

"The arrogance of your heart has deceived you...Though you make your nest as high as an eagle's, I will bring you down from there, declares the Lord (Jeremiah 49:16). Rather than ask, "What can we learn from St. Helens?", as many are presently doing, we would rather ask, "What will we learn from the experience?" Will we continue in our self-reliant, business-as-usual independence Or, will we draw close and remain still before our Father, and realize that He indeed is God, the maker and creator, the final authority, the one who casts mountains into the sea. (Revelations 8:8)

I raise my hands over my head and stretch. My back aches. Nick has set up his GI Joes all around the living room. He hands Sara a tank and tells her to go shoot the men in the corner. Howard and I have had deep conversations about whether it's ok to let your kids play war and with guns. In the end, what is half the Bible about?

War and destruction.

I pull out the sheet from the typewriter and hand it to Howard. He's exhausted. It takes a lot of energy for him to think and concentrate this hard for a prolonged period. He sets the pages down, opens the file folder with his left hand, picks the pages backup with his left and places them into the folder. We'll resume tomorrow, Lord willing.

CHAPTER 22

Howard's Journal
October 16, 1984

Acts 2:17-18
I will pour forth My spirit upon all flesh...I will in those days pour forth my spirit.
The prophecy fulfilled right now! I feel it thick and heavy!
Ties back into Acts 2. It is very real!
I am pondering in my heart (Luke 2:19-2:51) what is to be done with these- and wait upon the Lord. At this time, I have an unquenchable desire to get the Holy Scriptures into me and feel that I should pour forth my life into my family (as Jesus poured forth His life into the disciples). Perhaps the anointing I am feeling (and it is a physical feeling) is to pour my life into my family before I die, or perhaps it is for a greater purpose. I am "pondering in my heart" these things. I suppose I am under the anointing to die, just as Jesus (but what a death it will be!) But put away vain imaginings and leave it to the Lord. I am not my own anymore whatever the Lord wants to do with me, I will willingly do- I am a slave for Christ's sake.

Luke 23:28
Weep not for me, but for yourselves.
This happened at the crucifixion. "Daughters of Jerusalem, stop weeping for me, but weep for yourselves and for your children" (the Jews). My salvation is assured as long as I believe to the end. Rather pray for those whose salvation isn't assured!

I WILL ENTER HIS GATES

John 5:24
He who hears My word, and believes Him who sent Me, has eternal life…he has passed out of death to life.
A promise I was given about two to three months ago.

John 3:5-6
Unless one is born of water and the Spirit, he cannot enter the kingdom of God. That which is born of the flesh is flesh, and that which is born of the Spirit is Spirit.
I had to be born of the Spirit before I was able to enter God's kingdom. I was born in the Spirit. God is poured out upon me, in my week of revelations.

John 3:27
No one can receive anything except what is given him from heaven.

Hebrews 12:2
For the joy of it He endured the cross.
I never understood that verse, but death ushers up into life.
The Lord has visited this house; there is a heavy anointing upon this house (since October 15), so thick that you could cut it with a knife. I feel it.
I am experiencing a joy being with my family that I have never known before, that I don't want to give up. I have to realize that the Lord is giving these days to me, and when He calls, I need to return the favor shown to me by answering in a dignified manner, "Lord, here I am. Thank you for the days you have given to me." I can't hold on, knowing that they are given to me by the Lord as a special kindness. Will I hold on? I pray for the dignity to say, "Here I am" and mean it.
I love the Bible- its words are truth and life. Once again, the concept of words as opposed to written words.) Should the Lord call me home, I would have one regret- to be without the Holy Scriptures. There is something supernatural about them, especially when they

are spoken and not read. I never knew! I never knew!!

I thank the Lord that He has freed up me writing pen and thoughts- He has given me subtly of thought process this week- part of the heavy anointing! I have felt all week. I have been healed mentally this week- I really don't care what happens to the physical body, the way it looks- I have a lot to offer my family now that I've been healed mentally! All thanks be given to the Father- He has given me a gift which is more precious than gold! He has given me the gift of His Holy Spirit!

In regard to not praying hard enough for healing. God is not a puppet that we can control by the amount of praying we do, or good works.

Concerning the Anointing: A simple note- It is not something which I chose and work to continue. I want it to continue, but God the Father only choses whether He will continue the anointing which is upon this house, or not. A special anointing. I can't do anything to continue the grace shown to his household. All I can do is obey his dictates, whether or not he chooses to contrive to show special graces to this house hold or not! Concerning Note of October 19, 8th entry: Jan pointed out that the Holy Scriptures being opened to me will be no drawback,

1 Corinthians 13:12

Then we see only puzzling reflections in a mirror, but then we shall see face to face.

Then we shall truly have fullness of joy!

October 24

Whatever has been granted me doesn't operate because of any formula (i.e. the spoken word) but only because of His direct presence- He would choose to leave at any time, and I would not be able to get His presence back, no matter what I tried to do, unless He wanted to come back, I am entirely dependent upon the Lord and what He chooses to do. All that I can pray is that He is willing to stay in my presence! I am totally reliant on what He chooses to give to me. These are not just words spoken to make me sound spiritual, people.

1948-1984

I said that I was sure that something was supposed to happen in 1984- I based it at that time on the title of the book 1984- the consolation of Israel took place in 1948. This is a mirror image of the year in which I felt something was going to happen.

Leviticus. 20:26

You shall behold to Me; for I the Lord am holy, and have separated you from the peoples, that you should be mine.

October 25

My mind has been released from bondage. The chains that were around my mind have been shattered, broken away!

Mark 12:30

Therefore, you shall love the Lord your God with all your heart, should, mind and strength.

There is a freeing of my mind- clear headedness, especially toward the scriptures (but in all areas) that I didn't even know as was possible. Really! This anointing is upon this temple- all praise be given to the Father which is above. I refer have experienced such freedom of body, soul and spirit, cleanness of mind. Avoid explanations and vain conjectures- deal only in the reality of what you are experiencing and know that it has been sent by Me. I feel that an Old Testament anointing at least has come upon me. It is something very special and it is something in the physical plane.

October 28

This solid, thick and heavy anointing I have been describing is nothing less than the calling out placed on my life. I have been freed from the world! I am not of the world. There have been five categories of apostles: the twelve apostles; Paul, who as a lesser apostle, because he has not one of the twelve; false apostles; and present-day apostles. I believe I have been released, anointed by the Lord and freed to instruct the nations, which explains why I feel the presence of the Lord so heavily and why I am sustained with only four hours of sleep a night and feel fresh! I have been taken out of the world. He promises to sustain the man who has given up all that serve him. I have striven to do just that.

This is not normal to have the calling of the Lord placed upon one's life. Only special vessels are chosen and appointed for that purpose by the Lord- they are specially hand-picked servants. Grandma Day gave me what I considered to be a prophecy when I visited her home. With an other-worldly gleam in her eye, she said that I was a minister of the Lord. That's what I relish in- to have a standard placed upon me which is higher that the norm. I can't stand for half ways. Being a minister of God's word is the honor of a lifetime. We all need the experience of being released for the shattered world; the fact that I feel the anointing poured out upon me honors me, that He considers me worthy and responsible enough to carry a load. He to whom much is given, much is required. I feel that load is prayer on behalf of the local church, body, interceding on their behalf that He would grant them what He has granted me- the spiritual insight to see into the reality of the 4th dimension. If they can actually see that, then they will have no doubts. I Corinthians 2:16

We have the mind of Christ.

I have thought it was almost blasphemy to be quoting the Lord with as much authority as He must have originally used. I can't explain but supernaturally, I have been thinking more and more, the words of Christ, with just as much boldness and authority as Christ himself. It's life his very existence has transferred within me, and I think His thoughts- I don't need anyone to tell me His words because I already know His thoughts (that's just the feeling I have). It's like that- I really do need people to tell me His words, but I have that feeling inside that I am thinking His thoughts, it is very supernatural!! Once again, I have no way of explaining this except that He has transferred his very existence within my body including His mind (brain!)

and I now think His thoughts, during the hours of the day that I am engaged in conversing with Him.

Leviticus 6:29
Every male among the priests may eat of the suffering; it is most holy.
That's what has happened; the anointing I feel the calling out- I am a priest ministering unto the Lord personally.

October 29
Leviticus 7:19
All who are clean may eat the flesh, but the person who eats of the flesh of the Lord's sacrifice of peace offerings, taking communion, while an uncleanness is upon him, that person will be cut off from his people.
Not accepted- no wonder I felt dirty with masturbating-I was dirty, ceremonially impure, and still would be in sex camp, but for Jesus reaching down and pulling me out of the pit- that is what has happened over the last five months- it was a battle for my soul in the principalities- that's why such joy has been overflowing in my heart- I have been freed from the enemy- set completely free- Jesus loved me enough, cared enough for me to come to me and pull me out – cared enough for me to work with me for fifteen years. How he must have cried and wept over my very soul.

Luke 15:7
There will be more joy in heaven over one sinner who repents than over ninety-nine righteous person who need no repentance.

News Flash- A battle has taken place in the heavenlies and Howard Rea has been Set free! Praise his Holy name!
This is not symbolic as I had always thought, dealing with God- I just couldn't visualize. But God was Jesus- the Lord is Jesus- they are one and the same- the Lord was actually present in the Garden

of Eden (physically) and when he passed by Moses in the cleft of the rocks (physically) he was actually there! But Jesus is the working of miracles and never did the same thing twice in a row. He appeared in a burning bush and spoke out of it. Hard to believe, I thought- mythology. He spoke to Moses out of a cloud which settled on the camp (a voice from heaven is too hard to believe!) Jesus was actually present and carried on conversations with a physically, manifested voice. This was all revealed to me from my spiritual battle incident of last week. There was an unseen presence, but real nonetheless! I just thought previously that Moses did it all out of his wisdom- but another was meeting with him and giving him commandments, the Lord himself, Jesus himself. I never knew. I never knew!

I feel like there is a cloud encircling my head, a vital force, freshness and vitality of mind, cleanness of thought, that I never had before, even in the creative days of producing the paper. My thoughts are sharp, not muddled as they used to be. I used to have to write and re-write until I found the right words- now after brain surgery, they just flow! There is an anointing upon me. I have felt the glow ever since I started keeping this journal. I have repeatedly said "something is happening; I have been anointed" but I didn't know why or for what purpose.

I was stuck in the mud! And only by his sovereign will am I here today- I had nothing to do with it! I was helpless and defenseless! I didn't even know that I had chains around my mind and they would still be there to this day if Jesus had not come down to release me and set the captive free! I don't know where I stood before Jesus before, but I am assured now of my most precious salvation.

I have an unquenchable desire to ingest the scriptures, to the point of wearing down my body- not caring anything for the body, but only the scriptures and the meanings thereof. I will eventually run down, unless the Lord (did you know that He is really there, as the scriptures indicate?) unless the Lord sustains. The Lord will sustain for as long as He has a use for me. I was three hours late on my Decadron medication, and my mind- brain- started going out of kilter- it's a real physical problem, but the Lord will sustain me just as long as he wants to use me- after that, he will gently ease me into heaven, no jolts or shocks; the Lord is a gentleman!

November 3

The presence of the Lord left today- I was jolted back into reality. It started yesterday- I was in the heavenlies yesterday all day in studying Leviticus; I wept and had much spiritual insight that was necessary for my understanding of basic truths. I came down from spiritual heights in degrees; I felt I was being jolted back into reality when I blew up at Sara over the reading kit yesterday and started off today by blowing up at Kyle for five minutes before I stabilized. I was happy the rest of the day and boldly witnessed to the Pacific Power lady. It flowed naturally, from spontaneity of the heart, there was no holding back, a free flow of witness, I have never done that before. I knew I was back in the world. I realized Jan was as spunky as ever (love flowed the past two weeks!) but then it was a downer- I was jolted back into an earthly existence by having to deal with the world again. I said I was going to take over the bills again three days ago the Lord knew he was going to leave today and was just preparing me for the occasion. I'm not sure the presence of the Lord has left. I know I've come down, perhaps it is the afterglow.

Truly, I was in the heavenlies. Now comes the testing period. Will I obey. Will I do the will of the Lord? And I played an earthly tape tonight- examine yourself by Pastor Dennis after having said in the journal a week ago that I don't need anything but the Bible tapes- why settle for a man's interpretation you can get the real thing. I had asked. This journal is pretty much closed except for Bible study and insights.

From the time of heavy anointing my days were numbered (again I only say "yea, yea or "nay, nay" only the Lord knows for sure).

John 12:35

For a little while longer the light is among you. Walk while you have the light...where you have the light, believe in the light.

I will leave shortly, will you continue in faith, year after year or gradually be worn down through the years?

Luke 18:8

Will the son of Man find faith in the death?

But for this purpose, I come to this hour. A whole lot more awaits me in heaven than on this earth. The question is faith. It takes a whole lot more faith to give up a life than to hold on to it, because in giving up a life willingly, you are trusting in God's word completely that what he promises he will do. In holding on one is really not trusting completely. I intend to trust completely! So, as in the days of the Old Testament, it becomes one day at a time, literally, and if one takes his eyes off Jesus for an instant, he will fall. One has to keep his eyes on Jesus constantly to keep in constant communion and communication with Jesus. If I take my eyes off him just one instant, I fall. I win no matter what I do-if I stay in constant contact with Jesus, I win on this earth; if I die, I win everything that Jesus has promised, for which there is no comparison!

John 13:36

Simon Peter said to him, "Lord, where are you going?" Jesus answered him, "Where I am going you cannot follow me now, but you will follow afterward."

II Corinthians 5:1-10

Indeed, in this house we groan, longing to be clothed with our dwelling from heaven. While we are at home in the body, we are absent from the Lord. For we walk by faith, not by sight, we prefer to be absent from the body and to be at home with the Lord.

Adoption as sons in heaven- the redemption of our body is our glorified body in heaven. People have told us to believe in little hopes on earth but hope that is seen on earth is not hope, Paul says. Real faith is hope in that which we do not see in this life, counting as the truth that we will in fact be resurrected from the grave after our death. Now, that is the faith which Paul is speaking about in this passage, the big hope. Aren't all other hopes little by comparison to putting your trust in God's word, not for tempered matters which will surely pass away, but for eternal matters? We will never see with human eyes so long as we are alive because we walk by faith, not by sight. Only after death can we realize the full potential of what the Lord has for us, but we have to go through death first. The truth that the Lord is going to bring us out on the other side is faith and that's why I seek to please Him. Why we're here on earth is the Big Faith.

Matthew 4:1-11 (The temptation of Jesus)
In this supernatural attack, I never thought it was before, but I know so now, because I had one supernatural visit from that same dimension of reality which I have been calling the 4th dimension. Subtle, crafty, deceitful, cunning. The voice of the Lord came to me, as if in a prophecy, and said,

"You have been anointed, the anointing is upon you- you can pretty much do as you wish concerning the pills."

I had quit taking them. As I stood at the counter, I got troubled in spirit, and knew I had to pray immediately- I went into the bedroom, leaving Kyle and Sara alone, and started to pray. I asked the Lord, "Confirm this, put a seal on this if it is of You," and I no sooner prayed this prayer than I had to go to sleep. Two hours later, I woke up, and automatically went in to take my pills. It was an automatic action. All that evening, I felt very weak, just like I had been drained! This was an assault from a supernatural source which corresponds to what I call the 4th dimension. Watch out for it- it's real. I have certain obligations in and to the world, but I must never be ashamed to take time in silent or oral prayer, not putting it off for one moment. This is serious business.

Things I learned by having this attack: Satan is real- I can't see him being from the 4th dimension but he nevertheless is a real, physical presence.

Matthew 4:1

Then Jesus was led up by the Spirit into the wilderness to be tempted by the devil.

1. Jesus quoted the word of God. I will not operate on any other condition except when the Spirit of the Lord falls heavily on me. God's pure word is good enough for me!

2. Jesus was weak after forty days of fasting- physically weak but not spiritually weak. He was able to discern a spirit even though He could not see it. He could feel its presence and know that it was something real.

3. The tempter talks in near misses, but God quotes His holy word. Verse 6 is the one He used in me.

If you are the son of God, throw yourself down, for it is written: He will give his angels charge over me, and on their hands will they bear you up.

The prophecy given to me came quoting none of the Bible, but instead offers the promises of being anointed, so I could pretty much do what I wanted, and God would back it up. That's the same tact he used of Jesus "It'll be OK whatever you choose to do, He will bear you up, or He will give his angels charge over you". It just came to light who those angels were- the fallen angels. Do you think they would have born him up? No! No! Anyway, the Lord had already addressed the issue concerning pills to me from his Word in

Matthew 4:11

Then the devil left him, and angels came and began to minister to him.

I believe angels ministered to me as I went into my deep sleep. For two hours, Kyle had the house to himself, and nothing was even out of place. I went into my bedroom, prayed a one liner, laid down on my bed to pray, but wound up getting into bed and almost instantaneously going into a deep sleep. Ministering angels can't be seen, but they are a reality of the 4th dimension, a physical presence. I never knew!

Mark 9:7-8

At the transfiguration, then a cloud formed over-shadowing them. And all at once they looked around and saw no one with them anymore, except Jesus only.

The first time I saw Jesus he appeared for about five seconds, then I rubbed my eyes in awe and amazement and by the time I stopped rubbing my eyes, He was gone. Tonight confirmed that this was a real experience I had had with the Lord that my eyes were not playing tricks on me. This experience occurred fourteen years ago at UCLA –the first time I had gone to Hal Lindsay's Compass Light and Power Company. I wasn't even earnestly calling on the name of the Lord at that time- I was more interested in getting a girlfriend- He chose me over fourteen years ago. He was calling me- only six years later did I get down on my knees to call on the name of the Lord.

Is there any scripture reference indicating that Jesus prayed all night? I am under a compulsion, driven to ingest and digest the scriptures, and I'm going to do my part to forever push forward- it's only a matter of how much time the Lord will grant me this compulsion- as far as I am concerned, compel me on, Lord, make me a man driven to ingest the scriptures- compel me forth! I have been up 24 hours straight, and I'm not even tired- I usually sleep an average of eight hours a night; now I'm getting an average of five hours in a 24-hour day.

November. 24

I felt that the Lord had lifted the anointing from the house last week, I don't know exactly when, but certainly by last Monday. Phoned up Dr. Ward about the medication I was on- I was getting bloated around the middle and I wanted to know why. He said that *he was under the impression that I was only taking one pill every nine hours, not three pills every six hours. However, that's what the nurse had fixed up when I converted to the new program. Anyway, as soon as I set down the phone, the Lord, (knowing what was in my heart, when I said to myself, I'm going to get off these pills), immediately caused me to vomit and I vomited for the next several hours. And for the next five days, I was sick. Friday night, I got into the Bible again, I had had no desire to read it since the previous Saturday the 17th. And I felt compelled to write down:*

II Chronicles. 16:11

In the 39th year of his reign, Asa was diseased in his feet, and his disease became severe; yet even in his disease he did not seek the Lord but sought help from physicians.

Isn't that exactly what I was doing- seeking advice form the physicians. Even though I had boldly affirmed on November 12 that I am living in a world above medical limitation? And again, medical diagnoses don't have any weight with me anymore. The Lord told me "Permit it at this time in order to fulfill all righteousness." And yet, I found myself going against His word, and going with what the doctor had told me. I'm not saying the doctor was wrong; I'm saying that I didn't seek the Lord first! O, when will I ever learn? The Lord will sustain me, on His terms, and His terms only. My terms are what got me into this mess to begin with. And if the Lord's terms are three pills every six hours, then it is three pills every six hours. "Permit it at this time in order to fulfill all righteousness"

November 29

That is the game plan- to give up one's life willingly. If you do you will get it back more abundantly than you ever imagined! This is a prophecy given me by the Lord:

Thus saith the Lord of Hosts in a prophecy to me:

"Manna was gathered one day at a time- so too your life, your very existence depends on meeting with me each day, one day at a time. If you look past one day, I will be sorely displeased. For these are my terms: look no further than one day at a time; this is a command! This is your test of faith, to rest in me! Give no thought for tomorrow."

I Corinthians. 15:35-54
Thus says the Lord "Concern not yourself with things of the flesh, for the flesh will perish- only the Spirit will live."

Concern yourself with life, and not death. By asking, now you obligate yourself to do My will. Anything less, than doing My full will is less of faith. By asking, you put yourself in the position of Moses- one act of disobedience didn't get him across the Jordan. He delighted himself to carry out all My instructions, and he failed in just one! How will you fare?

Ezekiel: 1:1
Now it came about in the 30th year- while I was by the river Cheban the heavens were opened and I saw visions of God and word of the Lord came expressly to Ezekiel the priest and there the hand of the Lord came upon him.

I feel that the Lord has healed me and fully restored me to health. People want to see a physical body restored and healed. But as far as I am concerned, I have been fully restored. Don't ever look on what you see outwardly rather look on the inward that is what God is concerned with. I am being fully restored in the inward man. The outward man is really of no concern to me.

DECEMBER 10

All things are opened before me- explanations of verses, etc. When and if there is a certain time limit given of me by the Lord whereby all things are opened to me, I fear I will not want to live up to the experience of fullness in joy that I am experiencing of having the Holy Scriptures opened before me. That is what Jesus must have been feeling.

The Lord God of hosts says to you:

You must constantly dwell on Me and Me only. Should you hesitate for a moment it could be harsh for you, unless you immediately come before Me.

A moment's hesitation could cause a moment of wavering and doubt, and will go unchecked until you catch it, and bring it before Me. Think of nothing but the holy scriptures- My holy word- and you will be guarded be the promises in that Word; think on anything else and you will be open to the ways of the world- your strength is in the Word.

I am experiencing the same fullness of joys that Simeon must have felt in

Luke 2:26:

And it had been revealed to him by the Holy Spirit that he would not see death before he had seen the Lord's Christ.

After that, he couldn't have cared whether he lived or died. The Lord had visited him, had fulfilled his promises to him, and had been faithful to him. What more could he ask?

Moses, in the cleft of the rock could only look on the back of God- a front view would have been too powerful. I feel an unquenched thirst to digest (ingest) the scriptures, but at the same time feel I must draw back, lest I be consumed out of zeal for the Lord's house. So heavenly minded no earthly good!

CHAPTER **23**

Warrenton

"GETTING READY TO go?" Dorothy asks me. I'm putting on my sweatshirt and digging for my keys.

"Yeah, calling it a day," I say.

I look around at the Montessori toys, the mural I painted on the wall, the playhouse and tons of books. It's been seven years since I started the preschool. I began with day care and preschool for ages three through five. Then I added infant/toddler care. The next step was to add after school care and lastly, private kindergarten. I had thirteen employees, had been able to increase their wages to $1.75 an hour and had looked into health insurance. We had been able to provide care to over ninety children. "I've been successful, Lord," I say under my breath. Then am quick to think, not me Lord, but for your glory. What more do you have for me?

"Head to the car," I tell the kiddos. Nick runs out the door and races Sara to the front seat. An argument ensues. I put Kyle on my hip and head out there to try to create peace.

"She got to be in the front this morning," Nick whines.

"Sara, get in the back," I command. Sara stomps off and pounds the door with her fist. I put Kyle in his car seat and we drive off.

The misty rain surrounds us, just enough for windshield wipers. Why don't they invent some that can only go intermittently so you don't have to leave them on full?

"Mom, when's daddy going to get better?" Sara asks. "It's been a long, long time. I heard that lady tell you at church that you should just have more faith, like in the Bible. Just like that lady that Jesus healed of her disease. How can we have more faith like that, so daddy can get well?"

"He's not going to get well, dummy," Nick says.

"Nick!" I say.

"Well?" he responds.

I have to ponder this. It's a good question, but one that has bothered me all week. Can we muster more faith? Was everyone in the Bible healed? Was there really something spiritually we could do that we were missing in order for Howard to be healed? So when Joanie, at church, said we just needed more faith, what does that actually look like? How much faith is "enough"? The Bible says that if you have faith like a mustard seed, you can move mountains. We at least have that much faith. And this mountain called "brain tumor" hasn't moved. But wait now, if all it takes is for us to have enough faith, we should be able to determine the outcome. But that's not for us to decide, is it? That would be making God into a puppet that we could control, rather than the other way around.

No, it's not about how much faith you have.

"Nick," I say, "there are different kinds of healings. Sometimes God doesn't give physical healings, but gives us spiritual healings, which are much more important. And sometimes the healing comes when a person enters heaven. And there is no doubt, since your dad is a believer, that he *will* be going to heaven."

I turn down our steep, graveled driveway and into the carport. Nick and Sara pile out while I unlatch Kyle's car seat. He reaches up for me to carry him in.

"You can walk, young man. You don't need to be carried everywhere."

As I enter through the laundry room, I hear the beep of the finished drier. I guess Howard was able to accomplish something while I was gone. I set down my purse and unload the clothes into the basket.

Kyle climbs inside on top of the warm clothes. Nick comes through.

"Hey Kyle, do you want a ride?" and begins to push him and the basket into the living room. Kyle giggles with glee. I'm glad there are some joyful sounds in my life in spite of all the overwhelming burden.

"Hop out now so I can fold the laundry," I say. I begin to sort and fold clothes onto the couch. Howard is at his desk.

He puts down his pen.

"Been writing again?" I ask.

"Yes, God has given me so many insights. Ya know, if I had never had this brain tumor, I don't know if I'd have ever gotten this close to Him. Sometimes I feel overpowered by his grace and love and so many, many insights."

"I'm glad. Today on the way home Sara asked if we didn't have enough faith for you to be healed," I say.

"Where'd she get that idea?" he asks.

"She overheard Joanie say something to me last week at church about needing more faith." I shake my head.

"I have suffered loss, true. I ended up without a hand and a leg because of the paralysis. But if God had decided to heal me instantly, I would not be "good" saved. I am saved as through fire- I came up lame, to enter life- I wish I had not had to enter that way, but I am glad that I'm still entering into His salvation."

I start rubbing his shoulders. He turns and kisses my hand. "Listen, here's what I wrote today.

Perhaps by my handicap, the Lord is trying to bring great fear upon the whole church, to show He is still alive and in authority, saying, "The Lord if He has to, will judge. Judgment begins in the house of the Lord" to bring those who are in the house of the Lord into their inheritance. The only way to bring many (myself for one) into their inheritance is by chastising them. I was chastised for my own good, so that I might enter into my salvation. The suffering now for a little while will be worth the hardship when I receive what the Lord has to offer then."

"I don't think he's bringing the whole church into judgment," I say. "But he certainly has assured you of his salvation."

"Philippians 1:21-23 says, "I have the desire to depart to be with Christ for that is very much better." Sometimes, Jan, it's hard for me to even want to stay in the world. I can *taste* heaven. I don't want to leave you guys, but really, would you want to live in this body?" he asks.

I shake my head no. Because, for sure, I would never want that. At all. Ever. I look over his shoulder and continue to read his journal.

2 Corinthians 1:3-5
In our hearts we felt the sentence of death. This happened that we might not rely on ourselves but on God.

If you are willing to give up life itself willingly you will get the abundant life. Anything less than that, and you are placing comforts first. None of those men who were bidden shall taste of My supper because they put comforts first.

Luke 14:24
If any man come to me, and hate not his father, and mother, and wife, and children, and brethren, and sisters, yea, and His own life also, he cannot be my disciple.

I said fifteen years, and then I'll go- but He says, Come, for all things are ready now.

I look at Howard. "God is really showing you a lot of things, isn't he?" I ask. Howard nods. "He's kinda been showing me something about giving up my life as well." I sit down on the arm of the couch. Howard swivels his chair around to face me.

"Today, when I got ready to leave the preschool, I looked around and saw all the things that have been accomplished there. I'm feeling a nudge to move on," I say.

I WILL ENTER HIS GATES

"What are you thinking of doing?" he asks.

"I was kind of thinking of applying at Warrenton Grade School. I was talking to Nick's teacher the other day on the field trip to the beach and she said there were several openings coming up." Howard nods.

"Besides giving me a better salary, we would have insurance."

"Did you pray about it?" Howard asks.

"I've been in prayer, yes."

"Then fill out an application and see where things go from there. A regular income and insurance would definitely be good."

Howard's Journal

I always thought that a ministry was only to be supplying the needs of the saints. I have wanted a ministry that is directed more to producing servitude to God. So, I have been just trying to be obedient by following orders, thinking that only in this was I being a blessing to God.

Sometimes it is easier to evangelize than to give money. I worry that we will not have enough for our needs. However,

2 Corinthians 9:8

God is able to make all grace abound to you, that always having all sufficiency in everything, you may have an abundance for every good deed.

I would be disappointing God by my doubts and worry if I don't make every part of the scriptures my life.

I feel so frustrated! Monday through Friday when I get up at 5 a.m. sometimes earlier, Jan is up too, getting ready for school. Then it's my turn for the bath. One thing leads to another and before you know it, it's 6-7:30 and time to go or else Kyle is ready to go! On those days, Monday through Friday I get about ten minutes of prayer in the morning, to establish peace within my own heart, to be calm. It's not possible. On Saturday and Sunday I get up at 5:00 and have three to five hours to establish the day with singing hymns, prayer, Bible reading, whatever flows and it does flow. But, Monday through Friday is a different matter. Ten minutes of prayer to establish the day!

If I have been called out, and I believe I have been called out of the world- it is for a special purpose. I believe it is to intercede on behalf of the people. I can't flow carrying a schedule around in my pocket. It is 8:00 at night before I get any concentrated efforts at doing what the Lord has called me to do and by then I'm half worn out. Manna was gathered in the morning and it only lasted until the sun came out and melted it. I get to collect manna from heaven for about ten minutes. That's not enough for me, or anyone. What am I going to do with this commission the Lord has given to me? I see the need, I feel the need, to pray for those who are stuck in the same situation that I have been stuck in.

John 17:16
    They are not of the world, even as I am not of the world.
    I am not of this world anymore, unless the Lord jolts me back into an earthly existence.

Corinthians 6:17
    He who is joined to the Lord becomes one spirit with him.

CHAPTER 24

"JAN," HOWARD CALLED. "I'm out the door. Nate and I are headed to the jail."

Howard climbs into Nate's rig and shuts the door. Nate carefully backs up, avoiding our blue Datsun hatchback, parked haphazardly to his right. He guns it up the steep graveled driveway, stopping precariously to watch both ways for highway traffic entering onto Hwy 101. Someday if we ever have enough money, we'd plan to pave it. Right now, it isn't really a priority.

"So how are you doing there ole Buddy," Nate said.

"Right now? I'm feeling great. I always feel excited about what God is going to accomplish when we go to the jail," Howard replied.

Nate and Howard had spent long hours talking about "real" Christianity. What did that look like? When Jesus said to go out and make disciples, what did that mean? Howard knew that he wasn't going to travel to the ends of the earth. He had explored that route and the door had been closed. But what about Clatsop County? Oregon is one of the least churched states in the nation. Howard had his newspaper, but he wanted to do something more up front and personal. He wanted to do something more bold. He knew what it was like to be the underdog, to feel oppressed and hopeless. He knew that God could use those things to minister to others. And that led him and Nate to venture out to a prison ministry.

They pull into the small parking lot of the Clatsop County Jail. The chipped paint and crumbling bricks show its age.

"Here we are," Nate says. "You ready?"

"Yeah. Let's pray before we go in," Howard says.

Nate parks the car and they bow their heads.

"Dear Lord, we are so grateful for your salvation. We are so grateful that you chose us to be your servants. We ask that as we go forth to minister life to these inmates, that You would send down your Holy Spirit to guide us, to guide our words, guide our encounters, to keep our minds pure and not judgmental. Keep our eyes focused on You for your glory. Amen."

"Let's do this!" Howard says and gets out.

Howard and Nate take the steps up to the front office of the jail.

"How may I help you?" the desk clerk asks.

"We're here for jail ministry," Nate says.

"May I see your ID please?"

Nate and Howard dig out their wallets. Howard flops his open on the counter and holds his lifeless hand on one side to keep it open while he pulls out his Driver's License. At least it's still good for something, he thinks.

"Just a moment while we run a background check," she says.

They look around at the institution green walls. The bars on the doors. The No Weapons Beyond This Point sign.

Ok, please hand over your wallet, your keys, anything in your pockets. You may not take in any books with hard back covers. If you have a Bible or any books, hand them to the guard to be inspected before you enter. You may not take in any writing utensils. They hand over their Bibles to the guard. He flips through them.

"Come this way."

They follow him down the corridor to a set of locked doors. The guard punches in a code. The doors open where they are met by another set of locked doors. He again punches in a code. They follow him past barred cells to a room with several chairs. Two men in orange jumpsuits are led in to visit with them. The guard remains in the room, legs spread, hands clasped behind him, gun on his hip.

Nate reaches out and clasps the man's hand.

"Good to see you again, man!" he says to Bob.

"Yeah, I look forward to your coming."

"This is my friend Howard," Nate says and points to him. "He's also a believer with an amazing story to tell."

Both men nod.

"Sit down. Tell me about your week?"

"Not much to tell," says Bob.

"Mind if we sit over here?" Howard asks Tom, the other inmate.

"Sure," he says, lifting his shoulders in an I-don't-care move.

Howard and Tom sit across from each other, a little awkwardly.

"So, Tom, I'm not here to know what you've done. I'm just here to be a friend and maybe share some things with you that you haven't thought of," Howard says.

"What's wrong with you, man? You have some type of disease or something?" Tom asks, looking at his atrophied right arm.

"No, I have a brain tumor. The surgery left me paralyzed."

"Wow, that sucks."

"Yeah, it does in a lot of ways. But God has taken me through an amazing life-changing experience since it happened. I was just a normal guy, going to work every day, spending time with my family, pursuing my own interests and then one day, BAM! I find out I've got a brain tumor. Let's just say it's taken some getting used to. How about you? What would you like to tell some guy who walked off the street to come spend time with you?"

Tom snorted. "Well, I don't know. Obviously, I'm not here because I'm a great guy. I guess you could say that my life hasn't been all that great. My first dad left me when I was five. Then my mom went through a series of boyfriends, some who I called dad, but most not. I just figured no one would stick around, so I started doing things that got me in trouble. I wasn't much good at school. We had to keep moving because my mom couldn't afford the rent. She worked two jobs, one at a bar and she wouldn't be home till late. I was on my own a lot of the time."

Howard nodded. This was a lot different from his upbringing. Sure, they moved when he was little, but that was only once. And his dad was gone a lot because of his job at Lockheed. He guessed he was a big wig, but he never really knew. His mom was a high school English teacher, so she was home when he got home from school.

"My dad worked long hours every day. I guess I didn't really know him much either since he wasn't home much," Howard said. "Tell me, have you ever thought about what sins you've committed?"

Tom looked at him like he was crazy. He shook his head. "Every day, all day long, I think about how guilty I feel for the crap I've done."

"I used to think that whatever I did only affected me. That I could do whatever I wanted, and no one would be the worse for wear," Howard said.

"What could you possibly have done that was that bad?" Tom queried.

"Let me just say this: when it comes to sin, God says it's all the same in His eyes. There aren't some sins that are worse than others. That's a man-made rule. The Bible says that "all have sinned and come short of the glory of God." Even the smallest white lie makes us black next to His purity."

"Wait, so you're saying that my knifing someone and almost killing him is the same as a white lie." Tom shook his head.

"Let me tell you something about God. He loves you so much that He gave his life to redeem you from your sins. He is the creator of the universe. And that very same God is the creator of you. He knew you before you were born, when you were still in your mother's womb. Have you ever made anything before?" Howard says.

"Yeah," Tom says. "When I was in 5th grade my teacher had us make race cars out of CD's. I was so proud of that thing. It won several races. I even got a ribbon."

"And that pride you felt for that car, is only a puny little thing compared to the pride God has in what he created in you." Howard opens his Bible. "It says in John 5:24,25, *Truly, truly I say to you, he who hears*

My word, and believes Him who sent Me, has eternal life, and does not come into judgment, but has passed out of death into life. Tom, God is not going to take the time and energy to create you and not know you intimately. His desire is not for you to live in sin. His desire is that you would come to know him. He wants to be your friend. He wants you to know that he's the ultimate father. He has unconditional love for you. He will never leave you or forsake you. He wants you to know that you can be free from guilt. He gave us an instruction manual of how to live life. It's this book here." Howard holds up his Bible.

Tom sits there, forearms resting on his knees, head in his hands. Finally, he looks up.

"I never had a dad that loved me. The most I ever heard about God has been as a cuss word. And how do I know that he's real? I mean, I believe in science."

"I know from my month in Good Samaritan Hospital that there still are unknowns in the medical world, let alone the world of science. Doctors have done brain surgery, an angiogram, spinal taps, CT scans, taken numerous blood samples, etc. and I still don't have a positive diagnosis which they can treat. I am told that I have to come in for more tests, another CT scan, a needle biopsy, and possibly another brain surgery- before doctors can even make a diagnosis. Then begin the treatments.

The point to be underscored is the fact that there are unknowns in the world of science. Who, then, is to eliminate Jesus Christ from existence, counting Him nothing more than a "good man of high moral standard"? Who, then, is to completely cancel Him out because he is so "illogical" to believe in.

And who is to shun the claims of Christ Jesus who claimed to be the son of God. That claim directly made mention of the fact that He was of a supernatural existence, not a natural one. Quite possibly, Jesus' claim to be from the other side of existence could prove true. The point is this: don't eliminate the possibility of Jesus' claims without putting them to the test! After all, it is the scientific way of doing things.

What can you do to check out Jesus' claims? You can simply say these words: "If there is a God, make yourself know to me." This puts the burden of proof on Him. This puts the burden of proof on Him to do the one thing He can do to prove his identity to you. This puts the burden of proof in Him to reach across the supernatural barrier to touch you. It is up to Him to communicate to You. If He does not, then presumably, He is not there, and can then be eliminated from your reality.

The one thing you must do is to keep an open mind and be honest with yourself. When something happens- and it will, if you are sincerely asking in a non-chiding manner- don't shrug it off as being just a coincidence. Realize that Christ Jesus is holding out His hand of mercy to you. As the scripture says in Ephesians 2:4 *But God, even when we were dead in our transgressions, made us alive together with Christ.* Jesus Christ will accept us into his kingdom. All we have to do is respond." Howard glances over at Nate who's giving the time sign.

"One last thought." Howard says. "There's no way of knowing of His reality, unless He shows us that. That's what the verse in Ephesians 2:8 means, which says: *For by grace you have been saved and that not of yourselves, it is the gift of God.* Realize that God is reaching out his hand to you to show you his reality. There is nothing you can do. Man can't reach to God; it is God reaching out to man out of mercy. Won't you let him reach into your life? There's no other way."

Tom looks up at him. His eyes are starting to moist up. "I want that."

"Then let's pray together," Howard says.

"Heavenly Father, you are a God who loves us, no matter what. A God who sees past our sins. A God who sent his son to die for us on a cross so that we could be free from sins and have everlasting life, a life of only goodness with you forever. Show this son of yours, Tom, your reality. Show him your love and forgiveness."

"Tom, are you ready to ask him to show you the way? To ask him for forgiveness and to receive His love? If you are, then go ahead and tell him that now."

Tom says, "I don't know what to say."

Howard says, "Just say what's on your heart, man."

Tom begins hesitantly. "God, I never really knew about you. I think I believe you are real. If you really are what Howard says, would you let me know? I am sorry, so sorry for what I've done." Tom looks at Howard. "Do I have to say amen or something?"

Howard laughs. "No, you just hold a conversation with him. Remember, He's your dad, your best friend. Talk to Him like that."

The guard says, "Time's up. Let's go." The men stand.

Howard says, "Would you like me to meet with you again next week?"

"Yes," Tom says. "I'll be here!"

CHAPTER 25

CHURCH IS ALMOST over. The musicians have come up for their final song. I look at Stan sitting at the drum set, wishing that Howard could still be in that seat. I reach for Howard's lifeless hand. I straighten his fingers. His arm has atrophied and won't straighten anymore. Janet and Grant lead us in singing, *It Is Well with My Soul*. We seldom sing hymns, but this one touches a cord.

> *When peace, like a river, attendeth my way,*
> *When sorrows like sea billows roll;*
> *Whatever my lot, Thou hast taught me to say,*
> *It is well, it is well with my soul.*

I have to keep reminding myself that it is indeed well with my soul. I guess sometimes I get so caught up in the everyday mundane details of life that I forget to keep my eyes vertically instead of horizontally.

> *But, Lord, 'tis for Thee, for Thy coming we wait,*
> *The sky, not the grave, is our goal*
> *Oh, trump of the angel! Oh, voice of the Lord!*
> *Blessed hope, blessed rest of my soul!*

I have selfishly asked the Lord how long. I know I shouldn't be focusing on me, but on how much longer Howard has to endure these chains, being locked up in that body. Is it so that God can keep perfecting him before he takes him? Is it so that he can influence others before he goes? I've read through some of his journal. It's rich. I accuse him of being so heavenly minded he's no earthly good. But why are we here at all? Not for all the busyness in each day. Is what I'm doing really helping me or my family or anyone else get closer to the Lord?

The song ends. Terri and Tom come over and says they've brought a whole dinner for us- roast beef, potatoes, salad, blackberry pie. We just need to heat it up when we get home. I give Terri a big, gracious hug.

Howard is talking to Evelyn. She has had a debilitating illness for the past eight years. I wave at Nick to come. He's been sitting with his friends- too cool for us.

I walk down the hall and pick up the Sara and Kyle from Children's Church. It's so nice to have them keep the kids so we can actually listen and soak during church. Sara and Kyle tumble out, racing toward the car. "I get front seat!" Sara yells. Nick reminds her that Dad is sitting in the front seat. Once seat belts are locked, I drive off. Yummy smells waft from the box Terri put in the car. Howard is humming the tune for It Is Well.

"I was just talking to Evelyn," he says. "She is having such a hard time getting through each day. The medications only work sometimes. She's found herself getting depressed."

"That's not good," I say. "I wonder if you could start writing encouraging cards to people. You are really good at writing and the Lord has shown you such great insights."

"Hmmm, I guess I could do that. I can't go evangelizing or witnessing, very well at least! But I can very readily sit on the living room sofa and pray or, I guess you're right, I could sit at my writing desk and write notes of encouragement in letters. And, God most graciously gave me the gift of a heavenly spirit language in order to carry on such intercessions- I never knew there could be such a fullness, such a completeness, such a fluency of the heavenly spirit language."

I nod. I'm so glad he has a vision. What is it they say? Without a vision the people perish. We pull up to the house. Howard heads to his desk and pulls out a piece of paper.

Howard's Journal

1 Peter 4:1-2 Christ suffered in the flesh, arm yourselves with the same thought, for whoever has suffered in the flesh has ceased from sin- he lives for the rest of the time (in the body) no longer by human passions but by the will of God.

4:12-14 Do not be surprised at the ordeal what comes upon you but rejoice in so far as you share Christ's sufferings.

Let those who suffer according to God's will do right and entrust their soul to a faithful creator.

March 3, 1984
Dear Evelyn,

I was glad that I got to talk with you this morning. You are such an inspiration to me. I guess we who are "handicapped" need to stick together. Here are some thoughts that I believe the Lord has been giving me.

If you have not been purchased with a price, you are still Satan's. If you are bought with a price, you are not your own, but a slave for Jesus' sake. You are not "calling the shots" anymore- Jesus Christ is. And what He says to do must be carried out, once again, you are His. You are either serving Jesus, or Satan. There is no in between.

If we believe this- and we do, we are resigned to God's will in our lives. We are slaves to Jesus Christ and nothing more. If He calls on us to sacrifice our lives so that one person could receive life, we will consider it an honor, because He picked us (me). That makes me very special because He picked me to make the extreme sacrifice. Few people are worthy enough to make that kind of sacrifice, because they put comfort first. I am resigned to putting myself last and whatever the Lord says to do, doing it.

Hebrews 12:2

The author and perfector of our faith, who for the joy set before Him endured the cross and has sat down at the right hand of the throne of God.

The one last sacrifice to be made is death. If you are willing to make that sacrifice, you come into the kingdom of abundance. If you are not willing to make that sacrifice because of comfortability, you are not a part of the kingdom, and worth nothing more than to be burned up as rubbish. His way is joy, because what He inherited is much, much more. He had obtained a perfect state, and the reward of His perfection was abundant life. What more of a reward could you ask for?

The temporal is a testing state; to see if one is worthy of eternal life or not. We all have a free decision to make; if we put comforts first, we are not worthy; if we put sacrifice first, we are worthy of entering into the kingdom, but sacrifice calls for giving up your life to receive it back again over abundantly.

For the past two or three years, I have wanted to experience the purity of the gospel, but I couldn't put my finger on just what it was. But I have come to the realization (in my hospital bed) that purity is summed up in one short phrase- sacrifices. The purity of the gospel is no more complicated than that- giving up one's comforts for the purpose of putting someone else first. We should consider ourselves to be least of all sincere, to meet everyone else's needs first and then you'll find that you have no time for your own problems.

I thought "doing" involved some ministry- drumming, witnessing, choir. But it really means doing the word of God.

Live righteously before the Lord
Have a close relationship with the Lord
Pray
Praise

Loving God with your whole heart

Nothing surprises me now. I wouldn't be surprised if I went into the hospital tomorrow, but I will make my plans as though nothing has ever happened to me. I will live to a good old age. I love life too much to "go gently into that good night." Life is a joy if I keep my eyes on Him.

Do not grow weary. Keep up the good fight.

In Christ,

Howard Rea

Dear Toby,

I've been thinking about you this week. I know you lost your job. That is so discouraging. I've had you in my prayers that God will reveal to you the right job for you. Maybe even put someone in your path who will lead you to the right job. You have so many talents.

I think it was no accident that I read 1 Peter tonight.

1 Peter 1:3-9

Blessed be the God and Father of our Lord Jesus Christ! According to his great mercy, he has caused us to be born again to a living hope through the resurrection of Jesus Christ from the dead, to an inheritance that is imperishable, undefiled, and unfading, kept in heaven for you, who by God's power are being guarded through faith for a salvation ready to be revealed in the last time. In this you rejoice, though now for a little while, if necessary, you have been grieved by various trials, so that the tested genuineness of your faith—more precious than gold that perishes though it is tested by fire—may be found to result in praise and glory and honor at the revelation of Jesus Christ. Though you have not seen Him, you love Him. Though you do not now see Him, you believe in Him and rejoice with joy that is inexpressible and filled with glory, obtaining the outcome of your faith, the salvation of your souls.

For me this passage gives me hope that through the resurrection of Jesus my inheritance is heaven. I believe that will happen much sooner for me than for you, but as for you, you have been grieved by various trials. Our end game is to prove the genuineness of our faith. We should always be praising and rejoicing with joy knowing that the God who loves us and created us has our best interests at heart. Do not give up. Keep trudging on. Trust is not always an easy thing to do. But I urge you to keep on.

In Christ,
Howard Rea

March 3
Luke 12:35

But if that slave says in his heart, my master will not care if I relax, take a rest, for a few days. Letter writing is such a fatiguing job- I always have to have something new and fresh and vital to say. And praying! Over and over and over again! For the same request. Take a break from that, too. People will understand, after all, you are handicapped! (Loose translation in the Howard Rea translation). And those who knew the master's will and did not get ready shall receive many lashes.

I am prepared for death. I have said that I was ready to go home time after time. But I never really considered the possibility of having to stay in the world and live in the world, a slow lingering death. That would be harder than just plain dying. That would take courage to live this way for the whole family as well. That would take a whole lot more courage than just dying; a whole lot more faith too. And yet, it looks like I won't make my May 14 "deadline". Grant me mercy; grant me the whole family mercy. This has been a very disquieting thought- the thought of a slow, lingering death. And yet, if that's what it takes to purify and cleanse me from all unrighteousness, come Lord Jesus. Maybe I'll even have a more glorious resurrection from what I am going through in this earth, but I am only going to willingly cast it all at the feet of the cross and give it all back to Jesus- I don't want jewels in my crown, I only want the Lord to be my inheritance- that's not asking too much, is it? (he asked, selfishly) I don't want anything, but that the Lord be my portion. And that is going to take much purifying to burn out the dross. But, in the end, I get the Lord- I willingly give my life to Him. Amen.

CHAPTER **26**

Warrenton

"HOW ARE YOU holding up?" Howard asks me. We're in the kitchen. The dishes are done. The kids are in bed. His arm is draped around my shoulder as we lean against the counter.

"Ok," I say.

"I know this is tough on you. You never expected to be married to an invalid and have to care for him."

"Yeah, but we've gotten through."

"I want to talk to you about something," he says. I look up at him. "When I die, I don't want you to remarry."

I pull away. "Are you serious?" I ask.

"I want it to be only us." I pull away. I walk into the adjoining room and start a load of laundry. He follows me.

"Howard, I'm 32 years old. Surely you can't expect me not to ever remarry!" Besides, I think, you'll be in heaven and won't even know the difference.

Tears begin to slip from his eyes. I want to understand. I want to fulfill his wishes. But what about me? What about the fact that I have been through all this too? What about the kids with no father?

"Let's not talk about this right now. Maybe we should think of what you want to do before you go home. What's been on your bucket list forever? Do you want to take a cruise? Do you want to go to any other countries? Do you want to visit anyone in particular? It doesn't matter. We can go do whatever you want."

He gets a hold of himself and blows his nose.

"I guess we could take a road trip with the kids," he says.

I take out a loan and we buy a maroon fifteen passenger van, one big enough to fit an electric wheelchair, kids and camping gear.

We set out to see Oregon. After stopping in Eugene to visit my sisters, we drive to a campground at Diamond Lake in Southern Oregon. We pay the entrance fee to the park and choose our campsite. The kids are ecstatic to be let out of their cooped-up enclosure. I get Nick to help me take out the electric wheelchair. I know Howard doesn't really want to use it, but it's that or he doesn't participate in our walks or adventures.

We pull out the tent poles and lay out the pieces. The tent is laid out square waiting to take shape. Kyle runs over it.

"Kyle!" Nick yells. "Get off of there!" Kyle jumps off and finds rocks to collect. We finally get the tent raised, the food and camp stove out and set up. I suggest we take a walk.

"I'm too tired. Why don't you all go on and I'll stay here," Howard says.

"Are you sure you're going to be alright by yourself?" I ask. I'm getting weary. I need a little walk and beauty to restore my soul.

"Yeah, go on ahead." Howard's shoulders are bent and his eyes are vacant. His beard is beginning to grow down his chest. His stomach is protruding because of the medications. His back and chest are covered with zit-like boils. He's lost a lot of weight. Weight he didn't have to begin with.

I hold Kyle's hand as we hike down a trail to the lake. Nick and Sara swat at the thousands of gnats that are flying in the air buzzing around our heads. We have a hard time shooing them away. Just like all the thoughts swarming through my head. Really, how am I going to take care of three kids? I wonder how he'll die? I mean, what will actually be like? Will he die in his sleep? Will he have a heart attack?

Will he choke? I always wonder when I've gone somewhere if I'll come home and find him dead. I just don't want the kids to be there.

I check my watch. It's already been an hour. We should return. Who knows what being alone will do to Howard.

"Hey, we're back," I say as we approach the campsite. Then I notice Howard. He's sitting on the floor of the van with the side door open. He doesn't look up. He's got his hands extended, palms up, elbows on his knees. He's staring at his hands. In them are his prescriptions.

"Hey, do ya need some water for those? I'll get you some."

He slowly shakes his head no.

"I'm not going to take these anymore," he says.

"Wait. What? What do you mean?" I ask. He has to take them. He'll start having seizures again. We're a long way from the hospital.

"I don't like how they make me feel. I'm not taking them anymore," he insists.

I turn and walk away. I can't deal with this anymore. This was supposed to be quality family time. This was supposed to be our last attempt at family fun. Doesn't he care about us? I clench my fists. Who would just decide they weren't going to take the essential medications to keep them alive? I walk down the path. Driven. Why would he do that? Fine, let him die. I don't really care. If that's what he wants he can dig his own grave.

I look up from the road, suddenly aware of my surroundings. How long have I been walking? I need to get back. The kids are basically there alone. Who knows what kind of trouble Kyle will get into.

When I return, Nick is calling to me. "Where have you been? Dad needs help! I think he fainted or something."

Howard is sprawled out on the van floor. Nick helps me hoist him up onto the seat.

"Come on kids, we've got to leave," I say.

"What? Really?" Sara asks. "We just got here!"

We pull down the tent and gather all of our belongings. I have to get to where there's help. If I drive straight through, I can get to his mom's in sixteen hours. It doesn't occur to me that I should just take him to the nearest emergency room.

We head down Interstate 5 where I can go 80 mph. The sun has scorched the summer grasses brown. My thumbs are tapping the steering wheel. Maybe if I can get him to his mom's she'll knock some sense into him. Does he think this has all been easy for us? What about the strain it's placed on Nick? He's had to pull a lot of Howard's weight- bringing in firewood, doing more chores, helping change Kyle's diapers. He also ends up being the brunt of Howard's anger. Anger at what Howard can no longer do and expectations that Nick should fill his shoes. He's too young to have to grow up this fast.

It's six a.m. The last star is in the sky and the sun is on the desert horizon. We pull into a Denny's in Bakersfield. I'm exhausted. No, I'm dead. I lay my head on the table while the kids look over a menu. The waitress comes.

"Coffee?" she asks. "You look tired."

"I just drove fifteen hours straight," I say. I can barely look up.

The kids point to pictures of waffles piled high with strawberries and whip cream.

"Where's daddy?" Sara asks.

"He's sleeping in the van," I say. I know. I shouldn't leave him alone, but we've got to eat, and I've got to get some rest. And coffee.

I continue driving on I-5 past Magic Mountain to take the Lyons St. exit. Only a block more and we will arrive at Lucie's condo. The kids bound out of the van like cats cooped up in a cage. Kyle rings the doorbell repeatedly while Nick tries the door. It's locked. Of course it's locked! No one answers. He tries pounding on the door. Sara tries ringing the bell multiple times. My shoulders sag. Chiang, her Lhasa Apso is barking. Lucie probably doesn't have her hearing aids in. Now what do I do?

"Wait here on the steps and keep trying to get her attention," I tell them. "I'll head to the Dollar store and see if there's a pay phone. It's just around the corner. You'll be fine. *Don't* go anywhere!"

By the time I return, everyone except Howard is inside. Together we help him into the house. It takes two of us to help him up the steps. I'm thinking we should take him to the emergency room but know how expensive that would be. Lucie has already made a doctor's appointment. He's been throwing up everything he tries to eat.

The doctor prescribes a suppository and tells me how to insert it. Absolutely not on my bucket list. Howard is finally sleeping in the guest room. His old room. The kids are drinking a soda and watching cartoons oblivious to the enormity of the changes in their lives The TV is a rare treat since we don't have one.

Maybe a bath will relax me. I lock the bathroom door and slip into the soothing water letting it fill to the top. I need alone time. How did we get to this place? Tears slip from my eyes. My chest constricts, and I let go. Sobs gush from my innermost being. God, what in the world are you doing to us? How is all of this ok? We are faithful to you. We go to church three times a week, read the Bible daily, witness, give all our energies into serving and honoring You. We've tried to raise the kids as you would want us to. We tithe faithfully even if we don't have anything to give. What more can you want from us? From me? How much longer can this trial be?

I sit staring at the faucet, my mind a fog, caught in a netherworld.

I pull the plug in the tub. The water swirls down and I feel like I'm being pulled down with it. Swirling away down the drain. And then the Holy Spirit wraps his arms around me and says, "I know the plans I have for you. Plans for good, not for evil."

Jan,

Although it breaks my heart to say this, you are free to seek another mate.

From the time of my first seizure, I knew I should count my days. I speedily went downhill since that time. When I saw my arm and hand cramping up and was having so much trouble just walking across the living room (or the classroom) I wasn't happy with myself anyway. I felt like I would just be existing. I couldn't do anything for myself. And, did I mention that I love you?

You remember, from the first, I asked myself whether to get married or to become a disciple. There is a difference. I lost a degree or two by getting married. The decision wasn't too long on debate. Although, dying would be easier if I had chosen the other. All these tears that I've been crying- they're just because I love you all so much. (You could say it's depression, but that's just not true!)

I think my last days should have been spent at the Highway Missionary Society, because I have always believed that communities were more "right on" than churches. From the first, in Tuba City after we were married, I had that book on community living. That's all I had to go on- the first book I read after I was saved was the book of Acts. I think the Lord wanted that to be my pattern. I just got bogged down in church life.

I find, as I get worse and worse that you are having to do more and more. Eventually, you'll have to do everything (as if you're not already doing everything). And, I have to just sit around eating my heart out because I want to be doing something, but I can't!

The Lord has been good to me. He has prepared me for dying. I have left all that He has been telling me in the black case with all the important papers, along with my funeral outline. That's mainly music with scriptures. I know that God, in his gentleness and mercy will take care of you and the kids. Continue to trust Him.

CHAPTER 27

Seattle, Washington

FOR THE STOUTEST of people, it's hard not to get depressed living in the Pacific Northwest. We've now had 63 days of rain. Every day. Grey clouds. Wet. Gloomy. Muddy. Oppressive.

I start cleaning up the dishes. It's a little less work now that Howard has conceded that it's ok to use paper plates sometimes. I was leery of asking him, not wanting to get the "bad wife" award.

How had we come to this? I've been trying to work eight hours every day, come home and fix dinner, help Sara and Nick with their homework, pick up all the pieces that Howard is incapable of. Kyle is such a cling-on all the time. And then there's piles of laundry! Howard has lost some of his bladder control, which doesn't help. I wish I could just leave it all and go to Europe or somewhere far away! Oh how my life would have been different had I gone to France to study ceramics when I was pregnant with Nick.

Sara and Nick are playing on the floor in the living room.

"Give it to me! I had it first," Sara shouts.

"It's mine, you weren't playing with it," Nick says.

"But it's mine! I just put it down for a second," Sara screams. They start to tug at the toy, back and forth. Sara digs her nails into Nick's wrist.

I WILL ENTER HIS GATES

"Ouch! You little brat!" Nick yells.

I can't take this anymore. I go over to them, take both their heads and start to knock them into each other. Realizing what I'm doing, I stop and turn away. Nick's GI Joes are arranged at war on the couch. Suddenly I swipe my hand and wipe them all out, scattering them across the floor. I plop onto the couch and put my head in my hands. What did I just do? How have I gotten this far down? How long, Lord, before all of this is over? I plead. I don't really expect an answer. But one comes. *One year, my daughter. One more year.*

"Howard, you can't just spend every day in the bedroom staring at the floor and crying. What the heck is the matter with you, man? Where's your can-do attitude?" Rudy asks. He's trying to bolster him up, to pep talk him, to get him out of this eternal funk. Every day becomes more and more frustrating. He is either depressed, crying, or throwing something and yelling. This is not what I signed up for. A simple thing like trying to brush his teeth is beyond him. He's basically quit living. Why can't he just snap out of it?

We've moved to the living room. "Maybe you should take him back to the doctor," Rudy suggests. "This could be symptomatic."

"I don't know. I started calling around last week to see if there might be somewhere to move him. Somewhere that can deal with his medical needs. I'm getting to where I can't manage him anymore by myself. I just want this to be over. I want to get on with my life."

Rudy holds my shoulders looking me in the eyes. Then pulls me to him where I begin to sob.

Just about the greatest horror that I can imagaine (sic) would be to go back into the hospital for anything worse than a common cold (I'm exgerating (sic)- but not for surgery). I imagine the horror Jesus had to go through was the cross. Mine is going back into the hospital. They are not comparable, but that's the only comparison I can name up with to illustrate how much I detest the idea of going back into the hospital, to the point of sweating drops of blood concerning the possibility.

Drops of blood illustrates how little Jesus wanted to have to go through that experience. I want to go through the experience of going into the hospital for surgery just as little as Jesus did. That would be my cross. Having to feel the anxiety, frustration, treatment, etc. of another operation would be the death of me.

My thorn in the flesh is my brain. It is fresh for a while in the morning hours, but it gets tired along about now.

My physical condition makes me abnormal in that I am more so than ever reliant upon God for my every breath. He can snuff out my life anytime He wants to. He has control over me through my thorn. What's more, I know it! God controls me through my thorn. It is ever present. It's a constant reminder for me of my dependence on God.

Moses is still in heaven, but he wasn't allowed to cross over the Jordan because of his sin. I, too, am not going to be able to see the Promised Land (although I will be in heaven) because of my perpetual sin.

The sun is streaming through the living room window as I spread out a map of Seattle on the coffee table. I've gotten Howard an appointment at Virginia Mason Hospital in Seattle. Lucie has been pushing me to take him to a more specialized neurologist and why wouldn't she? She's his mother and is trying desperately to cling on to him. Virginia Mason Hospital comes highly recommended. At this point, I've looked at Mayo Clinic in Minnesota, John's Hopkins in Baltimore, UC Los Angeles Medical Center. Each long-distance call was raking up our phone bill. Lucie wanted him to have the best care. What were the logistics? How could we afford plane fare? Where would we stay? What if they wanted to keep him there for an extended time? What about the kids and the preschool? A paycheck of $600 a month wasn't going to buy that kind of options. Seattle was the closest.

I WILL ENTER HIS GATES

We've made it to Virginia Mason Hospital. We sit in Dr. Meyer's office. The traffic had been horrendous. Who would choose to live somewhere that they had to fight traffic on a regular basis? Marianne was watching the kids for me, again, getting them to school, taking Kyle to preschool.

Dr. Meyer's office was like all the others we'd been in. Tan walls, diplomas on the wall, window overlooking a landscaped courtyard. Somehow a landscaped courtyard is supposed to ease your anxiety. I suppose.

Howard is sitting on the exam table with his legs dangling over the side. Dr. Meyer starts in on what is now a routine exam to us. He takes a light and shines it in Howard's eyes. "Follow the light", he says. He shines it left then right, up then down. Looking for repeated movement when following the light. He holds his hand to the right of Howard's eyes and wiggles his fingers. How many fingers am I holding up?

"Follow my finger with your eyes without moving your head," he says. He moves his finger from his nose to Howard's nose.

Next, he tests for trigeminal nerve damage. He asks Howard to look at the corner of the room. He takes a cotton ball and brushes it to the side of his opposite eye. He watches for him to blink. Then asks if he can feel it. He can't.

The doctor continues by touching various places on his face with a sharp pointed stick. Then a dull one. Which do you feel, dull or sharp?

I'm watching every movement. Is he going to pass these tests? And what is a passing score? It's obvious the paralysis is worse than before. But then again, this doctor has never seen Howard before.

He hits a tuning fork on his hand and holds it behind his left ear. Tell me when you stop hearing it. He then holds it to Howard's ear for him to hear it. He repeats this then on his right.

He tells Howard to relax for a few minutes as he writes down the results of the tests. Howard looks at me. He's got his knuckle to his bottom lip and is nervously biting the skin again. I reach over and grasp his hand, his right hand, his paralyzed hand. It has atrophied, and it feels stiff. I straighten his fingers and massage them.

Now Dr. Meyer begins a muscle strength test. He touches each muscle group and has Howard push against him. His calf, his forearm, spread his fingers and try to keep them spread, his palm. His left side seems normal other than it hasn't been used as much since all he does is sit around all day. His writing hand is strong from holding the pen all day.

"Ok, let's move on to something easier," Doc says.

"Where are you today?"

"At the doctor's."

"Where is it located?"

"Here." Howard glances at me, like, is this the right answer?

"What city are you in?"

"It's in the mine above state," he says. I give an imperceptible negative nod. He's mixed his words up again. He'd done that after we left the hospital for his surgery. It was kind of cute then. Now it's a regular thing. And not cute.

He's searching for a name. I want to mouth Seattle but know I can't.

"What's today?"

"Monday."

"What month is it?"

He pauses. "March?"

"What year is it?"

"1984."

Dr. Meyer moves on to the Babinski test. He scratches the bottom of Howard's foot. His left foot is normal, his toes spread upward. His right foot, which is dropped, shows no movement.

"Ok, we're done with all the tests for now. I want to schedule you for a CT scan. I'll call down there and you should be called in shortly.

Yeah, shortly. Like in an hour as we sit on edge waiting.

I hand Howard his cane, which has advanced to a four prong. We walk slowly to the elevator. Cane clunk, hip hoists to lift his foot in the plastic brace. Cane clunk, lift. I push the button and we wait. I don't want to look at him. What is there to say? Is this the part in the movie where we say *hopeless*? Nothing good can come of this? And yet, there's still hope, right? We're still children of God, right? He still has a plan for us and together we can have strength to continue on.

They finally call us. I'm allowed to stand in the technician's room where the CT scan images will be displayed.

Howard is lying on the table; the huge donut surrounds his head. He's wearing headphones.

"You'll begin to feel the table moving slowly. You'll hear some buzzing and clicks and pings. If you should feel claustrophobic or need me to stop, feel free to push the call button," the technician says.

I'm allowed to stand behind the glass where I can see the images of the CT scan show up immediately. The first slide comes up. It's a right-side view. The first slice shows a small circle on the lower left. The next slide comes into view. A larger circle. The next, a larger circle. But the sixth and seventh slides, I see that the tumor is now taking up most of that side of his brain. My heart sinks. Any thoughts I had had that there was hope for recovery are now dashed. Of course, he's gone downhill. The evidence is all there.

Funny how you picture odd things in the middle of a massive life changing event. I see myself twisting the handle of a metal can opener. I have no idea what's in the can. The lid edges are wrinkled and sharp. That's all. No connection. No word of God moment.

And then real thoughts. Relevant thoughts. This is it, God, right? This is the end of the road. Only a small stretch to go. Last week we had rented the movie *Chariots of Fire*. Based on a true story. I had picked up the video cover and read-

Set in 1919, Harold Abrahams attends the University of Cambridge, where he becomes the first person to ever complete the Trinity Great Court Run. Abrahams achieves an undefeated string of victories in various national running competitions. Eric Liddell, born in China of Scottish missionary parents, is in Scotland. His devout sister Jennie disapproves of Liddell's plans to pursue competitive running. But Liddell sees running as a way of glorifying God before returning to China to work as a missionary.

When Eric Liddell accidentally misses a church prayer meeting because of his running, his sister Jennie upbraids him and accuses him of no longer caring about God. Eric tells her that though he intends to eventually return to the China mission, he feels divinely inspired when running, and that not to run would be to dishonor God, saying, "I believe that God made me for a purpose. But He also made me fast, and when I run, I feel His pleasure."

The two athletes, after years of training and racing, are accepted to represent Great Britain in the 1924 Olympics in Paris. While boarding the boat to Paris for the Olympics, Liddell learns the news that the heat for his 100-meter race will be on a Sunday. He refuses to run the race – despite strong pressure from the Prince of Wales and the British Olympic committee – because his Christian convictions prevent him from running on the Sabbath.

Hope appears when Liddell's teammate Lindsay, having already won a silver medal in the 400 meter hurdles, proposes to yield his place in the 400-meter race on the following Thursday to Liddell, who gratefully agrees. His religious convictions in the face of national athletic pride make headlines around the world.

Liddell delivers a sermon at the Paris Church of Scotland that Sunday, and quotes from Isaiah 40, ending with:

But they that wait upon the Lord shall renew their strength; they shall mount up with wings as eagles; they shall run, and not be weary; and they shall walk, and not faint.

Abrahams is badly beaten by the heavily favored United States runners in the 200-meter race. He knows his last chance for a medal will be the 100 meters. He competes in the race, and wins. Now Abrahams can get on with his life and reunite with his girlfriend Sybil, whom he had neglected for the sake of running. Before Liddell's race, the American coach remarks dismissively to his runners that Liddell has little chance of doing well in his now far longer 400- meter race. But one of the American runners, Jackson Scholz, hands Liddell a note of support for his convictions. Liddell defeats the American favorites and wins the gold medal.

https://en.wikipedia.org/wiki/Chariots_of_Fire

Howard writes in his journal.

1 Corinthians 9:23-25

Do you not know that in a race all the runners run, but only one gets the prize? Run in such a way as to get the prize. Everyone who competes in the games goes into strict training. They do it to get a crown that will not last, but we do it to get a crown that will last forever.

He looks up. Brushes his straight hair out of his eyes. He limps over to the record player and puts the needle back again to the beginning of the Chariots of Fire record. He resumes his writing.

I have run the good race. I have been a faithful servant. I have tried to live a life of integrity. I have given what I could to the poor, to the desolate, to the needy. I am ready, Lord, to see you face to face. I am ready to feel your embrace.

CHAPTER 28

Howard's Journal
September 15, 1985

He will be born again after he has died- he will literally be born again- raised again.

From the first, Jesus had the sentence of death upon Him; He knew that He was going to die, that that was what He came to do. And He knew that death would be a violent death. How did He react? Did He seek to prolong his life by easing up or compromising on what he had to say? No! Did He consume His life worrying how that death would come? No! Did He consume His life in scurrying around from place to place trying to find a cure or a way out of his dilemma? No! When He stood before Pilate and was given a chance to deny His claims- the equal to being given a reprieve in life, did He waver just a little bit? No! No! No! His time had come. He didn't compromise God's word even to save His life!

2 Corinthians 1:3-5

In our hearts we felt the sentence of death. This happened that we might not rely on ourselves but on God.

October 5
The body completely changes (science tells us) approximately every seven years. I am assured I am a permanent, unchanging, spiritual being with an ever- changing body and brain. If my body is changing constantly and yet I remain the same, it is certain I will survive the passing of my whole body at death.

"You must be born again"

November 30
Psalm 118:18
The Lord has chastened me severely, but he has not given me over to death.

Psalm 118:21
I will give you thanks, for you have become my salvation.

December 1
If you are willing to give up life itself willingly you will get the abundant life.
Anything less than that, and you are placing comforts first. None of those men who were bidden shall taste of my supper because they put comforts first.

Luke 14:24
If any man come to me, and hate not his father, and mother, and wife, and children, and brethren, and sisters, yea, and His own life also, he cannot be my disciple.
Fifteen years, and then I'll go- but He says, Come, for all things are ready now.

December 2
1 Corinthians 7: 8, 29-31, 32, 33
One who is unmarried is concerned about the things of the Lord,

how he may please the Lord. But one who is married is concerned about the things of the world, how he may please his wife.

December 4

One has to go through the state known as death to go to the promised land. There is no other way around it. What freaks people out about death is it's my ticket to the promised land. One doesn't inherit this land on this side of the Jordan (life) only on the other side- one has to go through the Jordan (watery grave, symbol of death, symbol of baptism, being buried to the old self) to come out on the other side "a land flowing with milk and honey". Why, O why, won't people let God determine what he wants for my life- what He wants, whether life or death, I can live with, knowing He has made the decisions. But when man makes his diagnosis with limited knowledge of the overall plan, how un-wise, foolish and vain for mere man to try to second guess the almighty.

JANUARY 6

It was not yet His time to die (John).

It is appointed for man to die once.

When it is time for me to die, that is the time that God has appointed. I will not die before the time that God has appointed for me to die. If I strive to stay alive after the appointed time, it will bear no fruit. If I try to have the doctor's keep me alive after that appointed time, I will accomplish nothing that will be recognized by God. God appointed His time, and I will have fought (striven) against His judgment like Hezekiah, who asked for fifteen more years after his appointed time of death, he lived physically, but he didn't live a peaceful moment during those years.

CHAPTER **29**

Warrenton

Howard's Journal

Immediately after I was showing a concern about whether I should be cremated or buried, the word of the Lord came in immediately with this: Luke 9:60- Let the dead bury their dead; but go now and preach the Kingdom of God. It was just like I was having a conversation with the Lord. I now know that I was!

HOWARD LOOKS UP from his dinner. His glasses have slipped down his nose. He looks over the top of them.

"I know what I want to do for my funeral." I stop mid-bite and look at him. "I don't want any of that everyone-is-dressed-in-black stuff. This is going to be a celebration. I will enter through heaven's gates and march into the presence of the King!" he announces exuberantly.

"What's a celebration?" Sara asks.

He smiles at her. "It's a party. And in this case, it will be a big party because I'm going home!"

Nick looks at him and says, "I thought you were home." He shakes his head like his dad has lost his marbles. And it's true, he has lost some of them.

I reach over and give Kyle more macaroni and cheese. He's going through a growth spurt.

"Well, I am. But we have two homes. The Bible says we are aliens on this earth. You know what an alien is, don't you?"

"Yeah," Nick says. "It's those little green guys with five eyes on tentacles!"

"That too!" Howard chuckles. "But an alien is a person who lives in a country that is not where he's from. We're aliens because we're really from heaven and we only get to spend so much time here on earth."

"Cool," Sara says, "We get two homes- I hope one is a castle."

"Think of it! I'll send out invitations to everyone I know. I wonder when I should do that." He puts his hand on his bearded chin.

"Invitations?" I'm embarrassed at the thought. He is in his own little universe.

"We'll start out the funeral singing *I Will Enter His Gates* and *Rejoice in the Lord Always*. And *Weeping May Endure for the Night*. And *Blessed Be the Name*. He looks at the ceiling. Oh, and don't forget *Emmanuel* and *Clap Your Hands*. He looks back at me. I want Grant and Janet Larson to sing and I want Rudy to do the service. I can trust him to put in a goodly amount of the salvation message. I don't want anyone not to hear how wonderful heaven's going to be. And I want to *see* all of my friends again."

"That will be cool," I say, one eyebrow cocked as I spoon canned peaches onto Kyle's plate. Nick and Sara are regarding Howard with interest.

Howard's blue eyes sparkle and are animated now. "Do you know how cool it's going to be to see Paul?"

"Paul?" I ask.

"Yeah, Paul- the apostle? I've got a lot of things to ask him. And Elijah! Boy howdy! And Abraham. Man, I could spend eternity just talking to those guys!" He pauses. "And best of all I can see our two babies! I wonder if they're still babies or if they've grown. Hmmmm. They would be about seven years old now."

I can't help but feel a little jealous. But instead I say, "And meanwhile, when you're having all that fun, you're going to leave me here alone to raise three kids- and one a teenage boy!"

"I'll put in a good word for you," Howard winks and chuckles. "Oh, and on my headstone I want it to have vines. You know, 'He is the vine we are the branches….'" He starts singing the song he wrote:

He is the vine we are the branches
Oh-o-o
He is the vine we are the branches
Oh-o-o
He is the vine we are the branches
Let's praise Him right now,
Right now
Right now
Oh-o
Right now
Let's praise Him right now.

"And where have you decided you want to be buried?" I ask. He and Lucie have been arguing about where his final resting place will be.

"I guess in Newhall next to my dad since she's already got the plot paid for. But we'll have the funeral here at Philadelphia Church. Well, I guess a Memorial Service. Whatever. I won't be around to know."

CHAPTER **30**

Warrenton

Howard's Journal
Most of all, I'm going to miss my family. That's the one thing I hold onto until my dying days. I'll miss Nick, and Sara and Kyle. And Mom- I'll miss Mom. One reason I'll miss you all is that I really fell in love with you all for the first time while I was in Good Samaritan Hospital. After I got out, I was going to change all my ways. I thought I would be all changed but I wasn't. I wanted to make it up to you all, and now I won't get a chance.

I'll miss all of the Lord was telling me from His word. I was really getting good at hearing Him for the first time in my life on a consistent basis, since my stay at Good Sam.

I think that the only way I will be able to not pass on the cynicism and pessimism of my mother, to the third and fourth generations, is to die. I grew up under it for twenty-nine years and by the time I get it all worked out, Kyle will have graduated from high school.

John 14:27
My peace I give to you, not as the world gives peace.
I am experiencing a peace that never have experienced before, ever in my life.

Matt 10:37
He who loves father or mother more than Me is not worthy of me and he who loves son or daughter more than me is not worthy of me.

I love my wife, daughter and two sons. Although that is not what the scripture is saying in this passage (from the context) it still has meaning for me. If I don't want to give my life when the Lord beckons because of love for my wife, or daughter, or sons, I love them, and not Jesus, more by comparison. Paul said, "To die is gain." I must have this perspective; that by dying, I don't lose wife, sons and daughter, but I am gaining Christ. I must keep my focus on Him and what He desires first and give second consideration to my family (wife, sons, and daughter). He's got my life in His hands; I have realized that. I haven't developed perfect peace on Matt. 10:75 although I know that this is the mind of Christ on the topic of death.

1 Corinthians 7: 8, 29-31, 32, 33
One who is unmarried is concerned about the things of the Lord, how he may please the Lord. But one who is married is concerned about the things of the world, how he may please his wife.

I wanted to get this down before I forgot it. This explains my hesitation at giving up my family. If I had no family, I would die a lot easier. But, since I have a family, I have to be concerned about the world, making provision for them after I am gone. And then, too, that explains the pull I have felt that I wanted to serve the Lord fully, wholly, purely, but I haven't been able to flow in this because practical matters always draw one back to the "real" world. You have heard of the man that was so spiritual that he was of no world good- when I want to put my whole self into the Lord, I find my wife letting me know of little things that need to be fixed around the house. And because I love, I want to do it, but that has always been a source of imbalance for me. I need to be unmarried to serve the Lord purely, but I don't regret getting married. I wish I could do both.

A NOTE TO MY FAMILY
John 14:1-3

Let not your heart be troubled; believe in God, believe also in Me. In My Father's house are many dwelling places; if it were not so, I would have told you; for I go to prepare a place for you. And if I go and prepare a place for you, I will come again, and receive you to Myself; that where I am, there you may be also.

I can see it! Hold on to that- it real!! Right now, I am weeping, because my family Jan, Nick, Sara, Kyle, isn't being called into this peace. But is being left with all the heartaches of the world. But, again, I'm acting on the supposition that I am being set free. Only the Lord knows.

By creating God in our own image, we lose. We cannot even begin to fathom what a glorious place heaven is, and because we don't know, we limit our picture of heaven to man's terms. We picture heaven in terms of what we know and understand, see, touch, and feel. But heaven is infinite, unlimited, no one can understand what glory awaits us. It's best to have God tell us, reveal to us, the glory in what heaven will be like. Whereas, those who create God in their own image won't ever be there! Truth is working on God to reveal. Trying to relate God in man's image is the lie.

CHAPTER 31

Warrenton

Death

I will enter His gates with thanksgiving in my heart
I will enter His courts with praise
I will say this is the day that the Lord has made
I will rejoice for He has made me glad.

I stand, stunned, staring at the empty place in the bed. The place that will no longer hold my husband. Lord, is this it? Is this the end? And then, an audible voice.

"Yea, though I walk through the valley of the shadow of death, I will fear no evil." I look around to see which one of the men had said it. No, it wasn't them. They were outside putting Howard into the ambulance.

"Yea, though I walk through the valley of the shadow of death, I will fear no evil," I repeat. "This is it, Lord, isn't it? He's going home, isn't he? He's going home!"

I throw on some clothes, tell Nick that Granma and Grandpa Knotts will be here soon and rush out to my car. My hand is shaking as I try to put the key into the ignition. I wait for the ambulance to pull out of the driveway and then shift into reverse. I realize I haven't put on my headlights. I quickly switch them on. My heart is pounding, and my mind is racing. I left without looking in on Sara and Kyle. What kind of mom would do that?

The ambulance lights are whirling. I notice they haven't put on the siren, but then, it's midnight and there really isn't any traffic.

What happens next? When I get to the hospital, will they keep him? Will he ever come home? And if he does, what other hardships will we have to endure? I'm only 32. Will I really be a widow at 32? And a single mom with three kids?

We pull up to the hospital. I jump out of the car and watch them wheel the gurney in. I want to follow him in, but I have to check him in and fill out paperwork. My hand is shaking as I realize how grateful I am for my teaching job at Warrenton Grade School where I have insurance.

The receptionist leads me through the double doors to where Howard is lying unconscious on the bed. Monitors are beeping, tubes are in his nose, an IV running through his arm.

I put my hand on his forehead and push away his straight bangs. I look at his long eyelashes jealously. All of a sudden, his eyes open and he sits up and raises his hands to the sky. "They're there!" he says. He's beaming. "The angels! They're there!"

Then he lies back down and resumes his comatose state. I take his hand. Tears run down my cheeks.

The doctor enters. Stands with a somber look.

"We need to life flight him to Portland," he says.

I make a quick phone call to Dick Knotts and let him know. I also call Lucie to let her know this is the end.

Tagging along with the medics who are rolling him out, I am glad it's not raining. I am surprised that I feel a supernatural peace and courage.

As the helicopter takes off, I hold Howard's hand and think, *you always wanted to fly.* I smile at the irony.

The intensive care room at Emmanuel Hospital is dim. Howard is lying on a bed with a monitor attached. A small green line travels across the screen and blips. Oxygen tubes are attached in his nose. His eyes are closed. A fan is blowing cool air over his red face.

"He seems peaceful," I say to Lucie.

"Yes," she says. She's holding his hand.

"It seems a shame to waste those beautiful long eyelashes," I say, "and beautiful teeth."

Lucie looks up. "It seems like he's hovering above us. Like he's out of his body." I feel it too.

"Maybe we should watch what we say. He can probably hear us!" What should I say to him? About him? Seeing him like this is so strange. It's like he's asleep, but in a netherworld.

Today is the day we've decided to remove the life support. The doctors say he is brain dead. That even if he revived on his own, he would be a vegetable. There is no way Howard would want that. Ever. And to be kept from going home when he's so close to heaven?

Someone is standing in the doorway. "How are you two holding up?" Rudy asks.

I nod. "OK. I think I'm ready to say goodbye." I look at Rudy. This guy who has been with Howard from the beginning and stuck it out. This guy who gave him advice, prayed with him, even gave him a bath when I couldn't.

"Thank you for staying with him. I just can't be here when he goes." I linger as I look at Howard, studying each feature. I kiss his forehead. I stroke his beard. I touch his lips with my fingertips. I think I should tell him something. What? Shouldn't I end our relationship with something meaningful? Powerful? I'm scared. It's like I'm peering outside of my body. This isn't like they show in the movies. There are no tears sliding down my cheeks. I'm not gut wrenching overcome with grief. I just feel- nothing.

"Goodbye," I say, "Don't forget to put in that good word for us." I walk out of the room and down the long hall.

I meet Marianne in the lobby. Her eyes search mine.

"He's gone?"

"Soon," I say. How do I describe this place I'm in? It's like being trapped in between two worlds. The one I can see and the one that I've put my faith in all these years.

"Let's go," I say.

She links arms ith me, and we walk slowly to the car.

"Do you want to call the kids?" Marianne asks.

"I can't tell them," I say. "I'll call Dick and Barbara Knotts and ask them to tell them." I didn't bring the kids to see Howard. I didn't want them to see him hooked to machines and comatose. That shouldn't be the last way they remember him. And I don't intend to have an open coffin.

I look up at the unusually blue sky and picture Howard floating up there to meet Jesus. What will it feel like? Is it instant? Do you just leave your body? Are you alone or is there an angel with you?

We drive to the Lloyd Center, the nearest shopping mall. Lucie wants me to buy him some new clothes to be buried in. I'm pretty sure Howard would think that was frivolous. Who's going to know what he spends eternity in?

Suddenly, as we're getting out of the car, a huge wind comes out of nowhere. Weird, I think and pull my sweater closer around me. I should just go straight to Macy's, but I get side tracked and blindly walk down the aisle of a toy store. All of a sudden, I am as if in a dream. I'm surrounded by a vision of Adam and Eve walking in the garden. Eve continues walking, but Adam is pulled up into the heavens by God's hand.

I stop and look at Marianne. "He's gone", I say and tell her what I just saw. She looks at her watch and then back at me. Outside the mysterious wind is just dying down. The clerk is adjusting the door that had swung open. "That was a weird wind," she comments.

Later, when Rudy tells us what time he died, we already know.

Howard's Journal

The Lord will sustain me just as long as he wants to use me- after that, he will gently ease me into heaven, no jolts or shocks; the Lord is a Gentleman!

EPILOGUE

Five Months after

I'M OUT IN the yard watching the kids play. It's an unusually warm, balmy October day. The sky is a brilliant blue. Sara hangs upside down on the tire swing hung from the pear tree. Nick is kicking a football to Kyle, who chases after it, still too small to catch. It's been five months since Howard died.

Over four hundred people attended his funeral, held at Philadelphia Church. We could sense Howard's presence there in the room, watching as Rudy gave a salvation message, according to Howard's wishes. He included words to Nick, Sara and Kyle that Howard had asked him to say- how much he loved them, how much he hoped they would follow Jesus in their lives, how much he would miss them. Janet and Grant sang as Howard had laid out the plan. People were so kind and loving. Somehow, I didn't cry. I couldn't cry. It seemed I had already done my grieving ahead of time. I did more comforting of others. So many people came up and shared how Howard's strength and faith had ministered to them. How they had watched him participate in the jail ministry. Or had written them encouraging letters, finding the things he could do, rather than concentrating on what he couldn't.

And then there was Howard's journal. Such amazing insights into God's glory and purpose. I had made copies for a few friends. This needs to be shared with others, I think.

I WILL ENTER HIS GATES

Sara runs up to me, interrupting my thoughts. "Can I go get the mail?" she asks, seeing the postal truck. I nod. She runs to the box and pulls out a handful of letters.

"Run and put them inside for now," I say.

My mind returns to Howard. Is he watching from heaven? I wish he were here to be with the kids. To see them grow up. To read to them. To throw the ball. To give them spiritual guidance.

An eagle is perched in the hemlock tree. It jumps and soars overhead. Its majestic white head looks down. The massive wings spread out and float on the currents. I want to be up there on his wings. I want to float on his back. I want to be nearer to heaven and Howard.

But those who hope in the Lord will renew their strength. They will soar on wings like eagles; they will run and not grow weary, they will walk and not be faint.

Tears start to fall. I had been doing all right, I thought. And now, here it comes again. I go inside and call Marianne. I sob into the phone. I can't even talk. "Just take your time. I'm here." she says.

I can't do it anymore. I didn't know it was going to be this hard. I never thought I'd be a widow at 32. She tells me that what I'm feeling is normal. Just take one day at a time. Each day will bring me closer to peace.

But I don't know how to be a parent alone. What if I fail? What if my kids are forever damaged by this mess? She doesn't respond. She tells me she'll come over as soon as she can. I hang up the phone and sit staring at the floor.

The mail is on the couch next to me. I pick it up absentmindedly. Power bill. Ad for an optician. Howard obviously doesn't need that anymore. Water bill. What's this? An actual letter. No return address. I slide the letter opener through and take it out. It's written on a piece of yellow notebook paper.

My Dear, Dear Jan,
 By now I've been in heaven for five months. I wish I could describe to you how wonderful it is here. Unbelievable!

I never knew! When I got here, there were people lined up for miles on either side of the street. (Yep, it really is gold!) They were applauding and smiling ear to ear. Two small children, a boy and girl, held my hand as they led me through the firecrackers that were going off and confetti was raining down. Boy howdy! You couldn't help but smile and feel warm all over. It brought tears to my eyes. And oh, all the people I knew! They grabbed me by the hand and hugged me. It was unbelievable. They were telling me all the ways that I had helped them. Stuff like sharing my lunch. Or giving a dollar to someone on the street. Or once, I guess I prayed with someone in the jail and later he accepted the Lord.

And at the end of the road, you guessed it, Jesus. Words cannot describe what it was like. To tell you the truth, I was a little afraid. No, I was a lot afraid! But then, he held his arms out to me and my feet couldn't take me fast enough to Him. (Yes, my new improved feet!) His embrace was like being wrapped in a warm blanket on a cold day. I melted into his arms.

I always thought I would be embarrassed by my life. There were so many things I hadn't done right. And it was so late in my life that I accepted Him. But truly, it was as if I had never done anything but praise and worship Him all my life. He showed me all the things I had done to further the kingdom. He especially liked the newspaper and is putting me in charge of the Celestial Chronicle! I also play concertina and drums during worship which is held 24/7.

Oh yeah, and the boy and girl that met me? Those were our two babies you lost! I don't know where she got the curly hair- not from me! And his sparkly blue eyes. You'll have so much fun when you meet them! I told them about their siblings. They said they already knew.

I see that you're doing a great job with the kids. I wish I could still be there to help you. Never grow weary. Never forget that Jesus does hear your prayers and is watching out for you. I know it's selfish, but I can't wait until you and the kids come walking through heaven's doors and join me here. I'm having the time of my life.

All my love. Give hugs and kisses to Nick, Sara and Kyle.
Howard

JOURNAL

The following are the entries of Howard's journal that were not included in the book chapters.

April 15

Ask...Seek...Knock...Find

Cease from striving and then (and only then) what you ask shall be added unto you because whoever heard of two loaves of bread feeding five thousand, unless tapped into the will of God first, and then asked is this the will of God.

1 Kings 19:4 He came to a broom bush, sat down under it and prayed that he might die. "I have had enough, Lord," he said. "Take my life, I am no better than my ancestors."

Elijah, after the Mount Carmel experience, sunk to dejection and asked for death. Then he was afraid and asked that he might die.

After the mountain-top experience of this afternoon, I, too, became dejected. The angels ministered to him, however, and picked him up again after his dejection. The second time the angel of the Lord came himself and ministered to him. Then, the Lord sent him on his way, but he wound up in a cave.

A great strong wind passed by. But the Lord was not in the wind. An earthquake- but the Lord was not in the earthquake (twice removed). Three times removed- a fire, but the Lord was not in the fire. The Lord was in the still small voice.

In spite of evidence that seems to indicate that I have a brain tumor, I have been given no definite proof that such is actually the case;

all is conjecture as yet.

And while the insurance company has continued to operate and base its opinions of what can be seen, I am operating from the perspective that, what cannot be seen, is just as valid a proof as that which can be seen, if it involves a total trust and complete balance upon God's sustaining power.

Faith is having this complete assurance (a sure knowledge) that God will bring to pass the promises written in His word, in spite of the fact that, at the present time, there is no physical evidence that such is going to happen. The Insurance company puts its trust in what it can see; I put my trust, my faith, in the higher plane of what cannot be seen, which is a practice more pleasing to the Lord.

Hebrews 11:7
By faith Noah, being warned by God of things not seen as yet, moved with fear and became the heir of righteousness which is by faith.
So too, I will put my complete reliance on the sustaining power of the Lord, and say with Shadrach, Meshach and Abednego

Daniel 3:17-18
Our God whom we serve is able to deliver us from the furnace of blazing fire and He will deliver us out of your hand. For, I have now been placed in the sustaining power of the Lord.
I don't view the life insurance policy that I recently applied for as a stay-above-water-or-drown-in-financial-ruin proposition.

John 21:25
There are many things which Jesus did, if they would be written every one, I suppose the world itself could not contain the books that should be written.

Luke 6:23
Rejoice ye in that day and leap for joy for behold, your reward is great in heaven.

I WILL ENTER HIS GATES

Luke 6:25

Woe unto ye that are full, for ye shall hunger; woe to you that laugh now, for ye shall mourn and weep.

August 30

I built upon the foundation with hay, stubble, wood and straw with bad attitudes toward certain people. The attitudes were never going to leave. My house was judged and burnt up, showing that it wasn't built upon Christ. I suffered loss- I would end up minus a hand and a leg. I am saved, yet as through fire- I came up lame, to enter life- I wish I had not had to enter that way, but I am glad that I'm still entering into His salvation.

September 20
St Francis of Assisi
Thomas `a Kempis- "On Death"

My last prayer is for a pure, holy church. Pure in that it seeks out needs to be taken care of. One which is not content with mediocrity, but one which goes after quality with all that it can; one which seeks after that church in Acts- whole heartedly. Because, let's face it, we have wandered away from that church and that example is the standard; my wandering away from the standard set in Acts brings death. But in getting professional, we have lost something in the translation, and that something is what is called heart. We have become too content with doing too little, too often. You're going to do something- anything! Then don't do it half-way. If something is important enough to do, then it should be done right. For example, the disciples in the book of Acts met together daily. Breathing, eating and drinking of the Word. I pray that we could live and breathe the Word, instead of just running through the motions.

September 27

How do you pour yourself into an ant so that the ant has perfect comprehension of what the person wants to tell him? He can't! The ant, at best, can just get a miniscule fraction of understanding from the person.

God had a whole other world He was trying to express to the twelve. His only vehicle- Jesus. Jesus spent three years, day after day, trying to teach of what it was like in His father's house. But, time and time again, He got so frustrated. It was just like trying to explain His Father's kingdom to an ant!

I got frustrated trying to explain what God was teaching me to Steve. I felt like I was talking to an ant. For the first time, I knew what Jesus had gone through. For the first time, I was able to put myself in Jesus' shoes and say, "O ye of little faith!"

October 17

I feel an anointing upon my being. I am in the 4th dimension, the dimension of the Spirit. I have been there for three or four weeks.

Mark 5:1-16 The story of the man with the unclean spirit.

Joel 1:4

What the gnawing locust has left, the swarming locust has eaten. The enemy did his best to destroy. Then I will make up to you for the years the swarming locust has eaten.

Eighteen years he chewed and worked to destroy, I know that bad awaits me. I have been redeemed! It doesn't matter if I live or die, nothing bad awaits me!

October 19

This is the bottom line- whether I look to the promises in God's Word, or whether I look at the situation. God has set it up all along- in Seattle, I was shown CT scans that looked dismal in order to test my faith. I have determined not to go in for anything but for maintenance. It's a question of whether I have faith in God's Word, or not- that's the bottom line. As long as I grip to God's Word, I will be sustained; if I ever look to anything but God's Word I will stumble. It is the test of faith God has chosen for me.

I Corinthians 15: 12-20

"But if there is no resurrection from the dead, not even Christ has been raised, and if Christ has not been raised, then our preaching is in vain...and if Christ has not been raised, your faith is worthless. but Christ has been raised from the dead."

Daniel 2:17-18

If it be so, our God whom we serve is able to deliver from the furnace. But even if He does not, we are not going to serve your gods. Our God is true; yours are not; we will worship the true God.

October 23
Malachi 3:10

Bring the full tithe into the storehouse.

We are under obligation to bring the full tithe into the storehouse- if we miss two months, we are obligated to make restitution to the Lord.

Mark 12:41-44

For they put in out of their surplus, but she, out of her poverty, put in all she owned, all she had to live on.

We will just treat it like one of the worldly bills, paying off $20 at a time, erasing the sum until it has all been erased from our obligation to the Lord.

Luke 19:2-9

Behold, half of my possessions I will give to the poor, and if I have defrauded anyone of anything (in this case, God) I will give back four times as much. Today, salvation has come to this house because he too, is a son of Abraham.

This was a prophecy given to me, later was the supporting scripture given

Matthew 6:25 -33

"Therefore, I tell you, do not worry about your life, what you will eat or drink; or about your body, what you will wear. Is not life more than food, and the body more than clothes? Look at the birds of the air; they do not sow or reap or store away in barns, and yet your heavenly Father feeds them. Are you not much more valuable than they? Can any one of you by worrying add a single hour to your life?"

Just rest in the Lord 24 hours a day.

The veil has been uncovered from my eyes- I can see into the heavens, figuratively, the ability has been given to me, (not I, but the Father has allowed me to see) to know the secrets that I always wanted to know but were veiled- I saw the explanations of them, but was unable to see, understand the reality- being in the 4th dimension as I am, the veils have been taken off my eyes, and I can see with spiritual insight (I have been given by the Lord). How long it will last, or for what purpose it has been given, I do not know. All I know is that it has been supernaturally given. It is a gift granted from heaven- I had nothing to do with it.

John 10:15, 17, 18

I lay down my life for the brethren. I lay down my life that I may take it again. No man taketh it from me, but I lay it down of myself. I have power to lay it down, and I have power to take it again.

The Word is cloaked round about in a shroud that keeps it hidden from view. Explanations are merely the reasoning of man, no matter how scriptural and accurate they may be. They are still behind the veil. Only when the veil is dropped does he see and he needs no explanation. He has come into direct contact with the Word of God- the Word being Jesus.

John 1:1

In the beginning was the Word and the Word was with God and the Word was God.

I don't need explanations from sermon tapes- when I have the real thing- the Word.

There are many things which Jesus did, if they would be written every one, I suppose the world itself could not contain the books that should be written.

October 24

A spiritual battle took place today, and it was so subtle that I came right out of Matt 4:1-10 (Jesus being tempted by the devil in the wilderness). I am convinced that prophecy should not only be based in the Word; it should in its purest form, be quoting the Word of God- all else is merely, again, man's interpretation of what God has said, when we have what God actually said in the Word of God. Why oh why, do we settle for anything less??

John 16:23

And in that day, you shall ask me nothing for whatever you should ask in my father's name he will give it you.

This is not talking about material objects, but divine insights. Whatever you want to know from the scriptures will be shown to you and the meanings of all these things penetrate your very being.

John 8:12

He who follows me should not walk in darkness but shall have the light of life.

A down payment in scriptural terms.

October 27

Lord and Jesus are interchangeable words for the same person. I just had this revelation in power when I realized that God, in Leviticus 17:11 was Jesus- the two are interchangeable, flowing in and around and through each other. God, who is talking in this passage uses the first person I and describes the purpose of which He came into the world- to make atonement for sins. Where else have you heard that before? I always considered it a doctrine to be accepted- the I in the 1st person *moves it into a whole different plane. These are basic, basic, truths that I am just discovering in power to show you who I am. Since the two are interchangeable, it makes no difference whether one talks about God or Jesus, they are both one and the same person being the trinity.*

Psalm 118:17
I shall not die, but live
And tell of the works of the Lord.

The Lord has disciplined me severely, but He has not given me over to death.
The gates of righteousness...I shall enter through them.

Psalm 121
I shall give thanks to thee, for thou has answered me. And though hast become my salvation.

John 5:24
He who has My word, does not come into judgement, but has passed out of death to life.
A promise given to me, instilled into my heart by the Holy Spirit.
Christ holds my life in his hands, my very existence in his hands. He can take my life anytime He chooses to, especially with the last set of CT scans, he let me view. I am under complete subjection to Him. He can choose to keep my life flickering, or snuff it out, by one snap of his finger. It all depends on my submission, on my obedience to Him. One act of disobedience towards God's revealed word (knowingly) kept Moses from crossing over Jordan. I'm in the same situation- one act of insurrection against the Lord can keep me out of the promised land or can blot out my life. He holds all the cards in His hands- it's merely up to me to obey Him! In short, I have to keep myself from getting spiritually lazy, as I did in the months following my hospital sojourn. After all that I still got spiritually lazy. And the parable that speaks to that is

Luke 12:16-21 especially. v. 19

I will say to my soul; Soul, you have many goods laid up for many years to come take your ease, eat, drink, and relax.

I can't let up before God anymore (heaven knows I did in the past) get spiritually lazy- or else the Lord may require of me my life. My soul is secure, but my physical life hangs in the balance and at any moment with a snap of his fingers, He can claim it.

I have chosen to put off the old man completely and put on the new. I made a free choice of my own will. I have chosen to mortify my old man. Last night, I made the comment to myself- no one else was within hearing range- that I hated the world. And I absolutely meant it.

Numbers 14:18

The Lord will by no means clear the guilty, visiting the iniquity of the fathers on the children to the 3rd and 4th generations.

That includes the 2nd generation as well- namely, Nick, Sara, and Kyle. The thought I had this evening was- does that mean that, because I didn't tithe during my wavering years, that sin of their father, (the Lord condemns the son of withholding the tithe) will be brought to bear of poverty on Nick, Sara and Kyle? Lord, be merciful to my children. Give to them the peace, love and joy throughout their lives that I don't deserve for I have knowingly and willingly failed you.

I just want to be pure and holy- nothing else makes any difference. It sounds from this that I am just about ready to go into the kingdom! I have an overwhelming desire to be holy.

October 30
Hebrews 11:13-16

These all died in faith, not having received what was promised in the literal sense; but having received it and greeted it from afar and having acknowledged that they were strangers and exiles on earth. For people who speak thus make it clear that they are seeking a homeland. If they had been thinking of that land from which they had gone out (the land of Uz) they would have opportunity to return from whence they came which was on earth. But, as it was, they desired a better country. That is, a heavenly one. God has prepared for them a city.

Hebrews 11:9-10
By faith Abraham lived as an alien in the land of promise, as in a foreign land. For he was looking for the city which has foundations whose architect and builder is God.

Abraham was living in the land God had promised him. He was living in the land of promise! But he lived, the book of Hebrews tells us, as an alien there in the land of promise, the land God had given to him. Why? Because, he knew that God had given him so much more; he was looking forward to the greater promise. The city which has foundations whose architect and builder is God himself, the Heavenly Jerusalem. As long as he was living on earth, he considered himself to be living in a foreign land; only in heaven did he consider himself to be living in his rightful home.

November 3
Luke 10:2
Pray ye therefore the Lord of the harvest that he would send forth laborers into the harvest.

I feel that I have been sent forth although I have physical limitations, as a prayer warrior. No less important, no more important, than any other job in the kingdom- just a job that needs to be done. No less reward- no greater reward- the Lord has commissioned me to His service for that purpose.

I Corinthians 5:6-7
Know ye that a little leaven leavened the whole lump. Purge out therefore the old leaven, that ye may be a new lump, as ye are unleavened.

This is what is going on in my life right now. I am being compelled to do this. I just have thirsting for righteousness, to get righteous before the Lord. I don't have any say in the matter. I don't want to have any say in the matter! It is a huge magnet drawing me forth steadily on one direction. To become righteous and holy before the Lord. He is the one doing it. This is what brought on the dialogue about being ready to be presented before him.

I Corinthians 7:29-31
Time is short, it remaineth, that both they that have wives be as though they had none.

Colossians 3:5
Mortify therefore your members which are upon the earth, fornication, uncleanness, inordinate affection, evil concupiscence, and covetousness, which is idolatry. If ye then be risen with Christ, seek those things which are above, where Christ sitteth on the right hand of God. Set your affection on things above, not on things on the earth, for ye are dead, and your life is hid with Christ in God.
I am being translated from earthly things to the heavenly.

Ephesians 4:22
Put off concerning the former conversation the old man, which is corrupt according to the deceitful lusts.
I am being compelled forth by the Lord to do these things.

November 5
"He who puts another first."
I put my mom first in that I worry about what my mom will think if I die before her. She would think that I was foolish not to go into the doctor's again. Not to pursue until I got it taken care of. I would think that she would say I told you so! If I worry about what others think I am putting Mom before Christ; I would be putting my mom before Christ if I worry what she would say if I died, rather than act upon Jesus' words.

Jesus walked out of a crowd who were going to stone Him for it was not yet time for His death. If I am going to sue, the one I would be suing would be God, not the doctors. I am not happy with what you have done, and I am going to get satisfaction. What God did was to give me a much closer relationship with Him than I ever had. He might never have saved me- If He didn't save me, He imparted a spirit of release on me.

November 9
John 4:46-53

Go your way; your son lives.

I believe by faith I wouldn't believe in any other way, that I have been healed. There could be a spot up there, but it's effect on me has been cancelled out; I am dealing only with the Lord now- if he can use me for five years, whatever period of time, He will sustain me for that long. I have no physical limitations anymore- my portion is the Lord. I exist to do His will! When He is done with me, and no sooner, will I go home. The Lord sustains me; I am living in a realm above medical limitations. I am now in the Lord's realm, the Lord's kingdom! Hallelujah! He is taking care of me and in my best interests.

November 10
II Corinthians 10:3-6

Though we walk in the flesh, we do not war after the flesh.

This was Paul. I knew a man in Christ about fourteen years ago, such a one caught up to the third heaven (4th dimension). He was caught up into paradise. Of such a one will I glory yet of myself I will not glory. For though I would desire glory, I shall not be a fool...I forbear, lest any man should think of me above that which he sees me to be and lest I be exalted above measure through the abundance of the revelations, I was given those in the flesh (limp and a crippled right arm) the messenger of Satan to buffet me, lest I should be exalted above measure. Most gladly therefore will I rather glory in my infirmities, that the power of Christ may rest upon me.

November 12

Should I die- I am not assuming anything that I am going to live or die; only the Lord knows what plans He has for me: I am resting in His will- should I die, however, I would have only one regret- now that He has freed me to freely minister to Him in song, in my heavenly prayer language, in a love for God's word that I have never known before, in a freedom and boldness to minister and with of the glory of God of the anointing that I felt when I was on the drama group as it carried the message into the streets rather than within the church setting. Christ meant for people to proclaim His name in the streets, you know. I would have to give up all of this (the things that I love doing the most- ministering the life of Christ) to lay down my life. I have no doubt that at least part of the reason why Jesus cried in the Garden was because He no longer would be able to proclaim the glory of God the Father, the same thing that plagues me! However, I have one consolation: the Lord is a gentleman. And I am dealing with Him and no other. He's not just a word, he is a person! I am dealing with the reality- He will sustain me. He has placed me on a realm above medical explanation- medical diagnoses don't have any weight with me anymore, for I am dealing with a whole new reality, the Lord's! I have experienced Him. Death has no restriction over me now, only the Lord. Only in His time and none other's will death be swallowed up in victory. But oh, I so want to tell of the joys that the Lord has shed abroad in my heart. I regret that I have but one life to give for my Lord. This is my only regret. Too, should I die, we have written this whole thing out acting only on supposition- I don't know what is going on, but I know something is going on! I have one more regret- that should I die, the family would have to stay in the world, with all of its problems and battles and struggles.

I lay down my life willingly, in order that I may receive it back- this brings a greater reward, brings a greater blessing.

We have to saturate our children with the love of the Lord that they will have no desire to do anything but to walk in the ways of the Lord; doing what is right in the sight of the Lord.

Deuteronomy 5:29
O that they had such a mind as this always, to fear Me and keep all my commandments that I might go well with their children forever.

I have been literally restored, brought back from the pit (he had me bound) to be the slave of Christ. You were a slave in Egypt and the Lord God redeemed you from there.

November 25
Christ hung on the cross and said, My God, My God, why have you forsaken me? He wondered if God was abandoning Him, if He was being punished. Is the brain tumor for a punishment or for a witness? I would say for a witness, but not for healing, but for endurance of the human spirit to know what is going to happen, but to endure anyway. But don't put assumptions on the Lord. Maybe it is just to get my mind completely on Him and not all this other junk that plagues us. Jesus must have wondered what was going on, as he hung on the cross and cried out- He thought he was being abandoned. And yet, He was exalted to the right hand of God. Sometimes I wonder if I am being punished by having been given a brain tumor, but on the other hand, Irene said on her last visit that God must consider me special that He would put me through this. Which is it, Lord? Are you just pruning out old bridges to the past, refining me or do you consider me wholly enough to undergo the same type of trials (though not as extreme) as you underwent? Which is it, Lord?

December 13
Even when it cannot be seen, there is life in a plant. Even though there is no evidence to show anybody that growth is taking place, the plant is growing, but you can't prove it to anyone.

The seed has been growing in my heart for eight years, although, I had no real convictions other that Jesus' death and resurrection. I could but "call the things that were not as though they already were". I thought I knew what I was up against. I was saying in my heart: I already know; it's no secret, but I'll play God's game. But the secret was, that I really didn't know what was in store. The seed lay dormant for eight years, and then, when I least expected it, it was there! And, when it came, it was nothing like I ever imagined it to be. It was a world of deep, deep, deep (deeper still) insights in what God's kingdom is.

December 14
It felt that the Lord's judgement was being poured out on my bad attitudes concerning the driving situation three years ago. The one I opened up to seemed to have such insensitive ears- could not hear what I was saying. Two nights ago, I had another thought about this. Perhaps- just maybe- the Lord was phasing me out of the drumming because He knew what waited ahead for me- an operation, and he was giving me plenty of time to readjust my thinking before the big day. The Lord didn't judge, the Lord wasn't angry. Rather, the Lord was being a gentleman once again. Rather than yank my teeth out suddenly, with a jolt, he was pulling them out with as little pain as possible.

December 20
I am weak- hobbled- physically, but strong, strong, strong in the spirit. Which, pray tell, does one want? I would rather (sincerely) be strong in the spirit, rather strong in body. Whose spirit will last forever, but the body of our earthly pride withers and dies.
One must make an act of the will to deny himself, to accept anything that the Lord dishes out. And that's what I did in Good Samaritan. I made it an act of my will to accept His will for me, whatever it was. I know that His will is best for me; His will is wiser than mine! I have lost my life for the sake of the gospel. I am denying my own interests in behalf of the gospel. And, I am willing to give up my life, physically, if the Lord calls me to do that, without bickering with the Lord should the Lord choose. I have given up all rights to my life and will to do his good pleasure at his bidding.
Get serious about the things of God!

And deliver them who through fear of death were all their lifetime subject to bondage. *This is where I was before entering Good Samaritan- I was in bondage because of my fears of death. The Lord had a lot of misconceptions to work out of me, and the only way He could have done it was to put me in the hospital. Otherwise, I would have gone on in my merry way being insensitive to the gospel's truths- I would still be on a diet of milk, but he Lord had something more than that- He was ready for me to begin partaking of solids.*

Take heed lest there in any of you be an evil heart of unbelief.

I had a heart of unbelief. I said all the right things, I had the right concepts planted in my mind, and I wanted to believe, but I didn't know for a surety all these things down in my heart. They were correct concepts, but I didn't meditate on them daily to know for sure those concepts.

We see that they could not enter in because of unbelief. *I had a lot of doubts, I was like one tossed by the sea, which fit into the category called unbelief- I bordered between belief and unbelief, which is not belief at all, but doubt. But the Lord wants whole-hearted devotion held firm, unwavering. I was not in that kingdom before Good Samaritan.*

December 27

Christ glorified not Himself though He were a son, yet He learned obedience by the things which He suffered

That is what happened in October.

Hebrews 6:4-6

For it is impossible for those who were once enlightened, and have tasted of the heavenly gift, and were made partakers of the Holy Ghost, and have tasted the good word of God and the powers of the world to come.

All these things happened to me- I was given enlightenment as to what heaven was going to be like, I flowed in the Holy Spirit, speaking in tongues. Fluently, I called this over and over again in my journal

"gift". The Holy Spirit fell upon me and my household. It is just like the hand of protection that fell upon the Hebrew children the night that all the Egyptian firstborn died- their doorposts were covered by the blood; therefore, they escaped the death angel. Nevertheless, we are warned that whoever tastes of the heavenly gifts and still falls away, puts the son of God to open shame. The Old Testament counterpart to this occurred when Moses was leading the Hebrew children across the dry Nile. God provided meat, and water, bread. Still they wanted to go back to Egypt.

I have tasted of the heavenly gift, been enlightened concerning heavenly things, been a partaker of the Holy Spirit, and have tasted in the world to come. Christ has switched the burden of proof back to me, asking Do I really love him? If I really do, just obey him. Yes, Lord, I will!! To him who much has been given, much will be required.

December 31

The only thing that will not be burned up will be your relationship with Jesus and what you have done to perpetuate the kingdom. It all centers around Jesus and one's relationship to him.

January 17, 1985

Messages for today: no matter how tired you get of fighting in the struggle (spiritual warfare) know that the enemy is trying to wear you down. But don't give up the battle. He who endures to the end shall be saved. Don't just toss in the hat and give up. This is open warfare; in open warfare, one is allowed only two choices; kill the enemy or be killed by the enemy. You can't get tired of the struggle- you are in it now, since October. If we only went to church to praise Him, if we never heard one word of exhortation or preaching, if we never got one thing out of the sermons, it would be enough just to praise Him. For what He has given. We don't need to get anything; man's greatest calling is to give all honor and glory to Him- we don't need to expect anything from Him but to be able to praise Him for who He is. If we got no more than that, being in His hands, that would be the greatest *gift He could offer, to be able to praise Him.*

Faith is not being able to see with the eyes but knowing- just knowing because you know- you don't need any physical proof- you know just because you must know

February 7
Romans 8:22
We know that the whole creation has been groaning in travail until now, and not only the creation, but we ourselves (I myself!) groan inwardly as I await eagerly my adoption as a Son of the most high God, and the redemption of my body.

Romans 12:12
Present your bodies a living sacrifice- do not be conformed to this world but be transformed by the renewing of your mind.

February 10
1 Corinthians 1: 7,8
You are lacking in no spiritual gift, as you wait for the revealing of our Lord Jesus Christ who will sustain you to the end.

February 14
Your life may be required of you at any time because of the new time commitment. You are not your own, you have been bought with a price. You could go at any time and nothing more. Your life may be required of you at any time after you have made the commitment. The commitment to Christ. Live each day as though you will never have tomorrow, your master may require it of you at any time. Your life and your world have to renege, because you have been bought with a price, and you are not your own. Count the cost. Get serious. Or throw it all in.

I Corinthians 7:29
From now on both those who have wives would be as though they had none.

I WILL ENTER HIS GATES

Namely, those who have given up wives (husbands) for the kingdom shall receive 100-fold back in heaven (for what they gave up on earth) Praise the Lord for a promise like that, but we have to go through humiliation on earth to inherit the promise of the kingdom.

I had two main flaws (sins) in my life before I went into the hospital. 1) attitude towards certain people and 2) problems with masturbating. They both have been gutted out. I want to thank the Lord that He made me fit for His kingdom in this way- I really don't believe I would have entered into the rest had He not taken me through that experience of forgiving- maybe I had received salvation, but I hadn't received sanctification, and the Lord knew I wouldn't want to enter in under any other terms- this is the one thing I wanted to do right, is have a right relationship with the Lord according to His terms- I didn't want anything less (I prayed this prayer in 1976 or 1977) the Lord is accordingly giving me what I desired. Oneness in His suffering and His humiliation but I will be guaranteed the heavenly kingdom.

You know I have been set apart for God as a eunuch when I can't have sexual intercourse. The word humiliation has been running through my mind these last two to three days. I feel humiliated in that I have broken out grossly on my chest and back and have a pot belly. The example of Hosea comes to mind- he was humiliated too. Go, take yourself a wife of harlotry and have children of harlotry. Hosea 1:2 Hosea was to take a wife who was a harlot and have children- bastards- by her. That was a humiliating experience. I have to live in humiliation, too, I have to live in this body. The only way I get any strength from what I am going through is to look at how humiliated Hosea must have been- the Lord told him to humiliate himself by taking a harlot wife. He had to live with the knowledge that she was out with a different man every night, playing around, while he was trying to live a life unto God.

February 19

I knew what I was supposed to be doing, but I didn't know how God felt about it, because I didn't know God the Father. I knew there was a standard to be kept, but that's all I knew, because I only partially believed in God (he was more of a concept, not a person). So, I couldn't relate to any feelings God had toward sin, because He was only a concept, not a flesh-and-blood person. He couldn't have feelings, He couldn't be frustrated with His people because He was only a concept. I know now that He is the first person of the trinity. He is a person, subject to all the feelings that people have.

I am a Gentile- I am completely ignorant of God's laws given to the Jews, and I should know them, if I truly want to know God in His fullness, and I do!

What Satan intended for evil, God used for good- He saved my soul and put a fire within me.

I had eyes but didn't see, had ears but didn't listen- before my seizure. I heard the Holy Spirit talking, but I didn't listen to Him. How was I any different from Israel? Of whom God says- how can I pardon you? I didn't give heed to the Holy Spirit's words.

February 26

The only way to pray perfectly in the will of God is to pray in the Spirit. I have been having experiences where I will be praying in English, but I won't be able to tell you what I prayed when I finish the prayer. At other times, I pray in my Spirit language, this removes me completely from what is being said- I know this prayer is in God's will, because He is praying, although I don't know what He is praying- But I do know that I would rather be in God's will no matter what He is praying, than to take the chance of being out of God's will and claiming promises that are out of God's will. I don't have any control over what He is praying, and I have to go on faith that what is being prayed is intelligible, makes sense and is in the will of God without faith it is impossible to please God.

The book of Zechariah shows how it will be in the heavenly Jerusalem- peace, peace, peace, peace. In which to lay all my weary struggles down (although the Lord has pretty much done that for me, given me rest from my tormentor) and just be at rest- not to have burdens any longer. Behold, thy king cometh unto thee.

February 28

This is not a test of my will power. This is a test of my faith! And if I die, I won't die doubting, wavering. I won't at least end my life on a doubt. I won't have the last note played in my life be a doubting note, a wavering note.

11 Corinthians 12:7-10

My grace is sufficient for you, for my power is made perfect in weakness. I will all the more gladly boast of my weaknesses, that the power of God may rest upon me.

II Corinthians 12:20

I fear that, when I come to you, I will find quarreling, jealousy, anger, selfishness, slander, gossip, conceit, disorder.

I was stuck in this trap of being a carnal Christian- although I didn't see myself as being one- I got into the trap of looking at others, not at myself (because I was already saved) I didn't use the Word for what it was meant to be used for- namely judging myself- but was rather using it to judge others. I had the same junk in my life that I was telling others to get out of their lives. I was using the Word of life to judge others, but I wasn't using it to judge myself, which was the main reason it was revealed to me.

Jeremiah 23:16-17

Do not listen to the words of the prophets they speak vision of their own minds, not from the mouth of the Lord.

The prophets of today are telling me to be healed- that nothing short of that will be considered to be a healing- they look on the physical only, not what has happened spiritually. Do not listen to the words of the prophets who prophecy. Rather, listen to the Lord, spend your energy in this pursuit.

Jeremiah 23:21

I did not send the prophets

I did not speak to them, yet they prophesied,
But if they had stood in my council, they would have proclaimed my Word.

True Christianity is serving the Lord with one's whole heart, not just half a heart. I praise the Lord that I am in a congregation where this is done- I feel the flow of the Spirit- you don't know how long it has been, I can feel the flow of the Spirit- waking in your midst.

April 1, 1985

(Typed up and given to people on Easter one month before Howard died.)

There are still unknowns in the world of scientific fact. So, quite possibly, the claims of Jesus Christ to be from the other side of existence could prove to be true. Who is to shun unequivocally His claims to be the very Son of God in the flesh? That claim presupposed that He was of a supernatural existence, not a natural one.

If you doubt His claim, transfer the burden of proof to Him. It then becomes His responsibility to communicate and prove His reality to you. If He does not do this, then presumable, He is not there and can be eliminated from your reality.

But, if He does reach across from the other side, be honest with yourself and admit that what is happening isn't just a coincidence. Rather, realize that Christ Jesus, out of His mercy, is reaching out to communicate His reality to you, and love Him for taking the time and making the effort to do so.

And, know this for a certainty: that by showing you His love, He has transferred the burden of proof back to you by asking, "Do you really love Me?" If you do, then choose to do His will yet one more day. If this is the first time you have seriously considered the issue, then, please take His yoke upon you and learn of Him, for His yoke is easy, and His burden is light. (Matt. 12:30)

April 17

Prayers I have prayed (so that when they happen, I will not walk hesitantly, or begrudges the Lord):

I WILL ENTER HIS GATES

I prayed that the Lord would do with me as He wills in this life, so that He could present me "blameless" before the King in the afterlife.

I prayed that the Lord would vent His displeasure upon me if I spoke words that didn't come from His mouth.

END OF JOURNAL

LETTER TO LUCIE, (Howard's mom)

> I have a lot of things to tell you concerning what has been happening to me lately. Very, very, VERY spiritual things- I really don't know what is happening, except that the Lord is getting ready to call me home. For one thing, for instance, I feel like I am walking more in the spiritual world than in the earthly world- I am being translated from worldly things to the heavenly, and that's not just a cliché. And, Jesus although I can't see Him, is very present, IS very real- He is alive (always a cliché before, but I can see him by sensing him). When you come up, I doubt I'll be able to talk about anything else. He IS REAL!! I have a premonition that I am being called in to the heavens, where fullness of joy awaits me. Or that I have been, or am being, completely healed, anyway, something very spiritual is happening. Now, we see only puzzling reflections in a mirror; but then we shall see face to face. My knowledge now is partial; then it will be whole. 1 Corinthians 12:12
>
> If my premonition is accurate, don't mourn over me- I will be happy; rather, pray for Jan, Nick, Sara, and Kyle- they will still be in the world, with all of its problems. And, once again, heaven is a very physical place, in a different realm perhaps, but just as physical as the earth. This has been revealed to me,
>
> Your loving son- more in December.
> Howard

October 11, 1978

I feel victorious about all that Marriage Encounter has opened up for us. I believe that we have both learned that our relationship- anything involving commitment- is work. So, whatever we commit ourselves to, will be work.

Having gotten this frame of mind, I have been able to branch out into other areas of commitment that I feel I can be victorious in, just because of what we learned at Marriage Encounter. I have decided to read a book all the way through before starting another, praying at 5:30 each morning, cooking. I feel especially pleased at how we are handling discussions about Nick- weekly, on Sunday, and working together, because we both feel the need. It has helped our relationship with him.

We need to commit ourselves to get a topic each night for the next morning.

I like praying in the morning. It opens up time to be with family in evening- or to walk and be with Nick in the evening.

We have felt victory a little at a time, and it is holding up for bigger victories for us as a family and individually.

October 8

Memories of holidays

Halloween- there are several Halloweens I remember. When we lived in California, I dressed up as a clown and a neighbor was taking pictures of all the trick-or-treaters. He had a whole set-up but wasn't a professional. Anyway, he took pictures that were really in a professional manner.

The first Halloween I remember was also in California. I dressed up as Zorro. I had a black cape and I used a curtain rod as my sword. I wore all black clothing. What a dude.

In Reno, my friends and I walked all over the place, covering neighborhoods separated by two or so miles. I had one of those realistic rubber masks. It was a pirate mask, with only one eye. The other eye was covered. Boy was it ever sweaty inside that mask.

I WILL ENTER HIS GATES

The year before I met you, I had treats to give out in Tuba City. It was all gone by 8:15. I started giving out some of my own food then. I finally wound up giving away some of my records. Boy, the kids just wouldn't stop coming.

October 20
We've got to remind each other. We're got to realize that, if what we plan to do is important to be doing, then we must do it consistently and that it is important enough to be done right.

December 8
Lord in the name of Jesus, I come against the strongholds Satan has erected in the mind of ___. I cast down those strongholds and every high thing in that mind which exalts itself against the knowledge of God, and I release that mind to obedience to Christ. I loose it to be reconciled to God. Amen

Things I need to purge from my life:
1st
Lust
Fear
Self-pity
2nd
Rejection
Clumsy
Resentment
Bitterness
Unforgiveness
Hatred
Depression
Timidity
Fear of man
Occult spirits
Mind control
Angers

JAN REA JOHNSON

Fits
Tantrums
Rage
Violence
Yoga
Failure

Book Club Questions

(Chapter 4)
- Has anything supernatural ever happened to you? Describe it.
- Is it ok to have sex before you're married?
- Why does God hate divorce? Why does he prefer that we not enter into premarital sexual relationships?

(Chapter 10)
- Has anyone ever made you feel uncomfortable in their touch? How did you handle it? Have you had release? Have you asked forgiveness? Have you forgiven the perpetrator?

(Chapter 10, 11)
- Howard struggled with finding the job that God wanted for him. Do you ever feel like you're not where God wants you to be?

(Chapter 12)
- How do you know where to turn when God closes doors?

(Chapters 14-16)
- How do you get through trials? What helps you the most? What gives you perspective?
- How does having trials affect your relationship with others in your family?

At work? At church?
- When you are at your weakest, what gives you strength?
- How can you be an encourager to others who struggle?
- What are the "right" words to say when you see someone struggling?
- Why are we sometimes afraid to get close to someone who is going through struggles or is near death?

(Chapter 18)
- What are your thoughts on tithing? Is it an if/then? If I tithe, God will reward me?
- When have you been at your lowest and God has provided for you? Has there ever been a time when God has placed someone on your heart to meet their need?

(Chapter 21)
- Is it ok to sue for malpractice?
- Do you agree with Howard that if you are not brought to your lowest, you don't enter into a deep relationship with God? Can you share a time when this has been your experience?

(Chapter 29)
- If you died tonight, where would you go? How do you know?
- How can you prepare yourself for Heaven?
- If you knew you only have a few years left to live, what would you do? How would you change your life? Or are you satisfied where you are?

Friends, there are tough times in our walk. Sometimes we think we've got it all together and life is smooth rolling. Then all of a sudden, we get a whammy. God never leaves us. It may feel like it sometimes. We may doubt that He's there or that He truly has our best interest at heart. But believe it. He does. He loves you dearly. You never know at the moment how He is working in the background to put things in place for His ultimate plan for your life.

Immerse yourself in the Word. Look at the lives of Ruth, Esther, or Joseph. God had an ultimate plan for each of them in His big purpose, but it sure didn't look that way to them when they were in the midst of their trials. Trust Him. Surround yourselves by others who trust Him and can buoy you up. Life wasn't meant to be lived alone to work out our sorrows by ourselves.

I know the plans I have for you, declares the Lord, plans to prosper you and not to harm you. Plans to give you a hope and a future. Jeremiah 29:11

Acknowledgments

THIS BOOK HAS taken many years to write. I began the week after Howard's death. Thank you to Howard for his journal and leaving it for the world to appreciate.

I especially want to thank my faithful friend Marianne Swanson, who was there for me from the beginning and plowed through with a pen in hand reading this manuscript. Friends like her are hard to find.

A special thank you to all those mentioned in the book and those who were not, who spent time on their knees for Howard and our family. Without their love and help, it would have been a much rougher time.

And mostly, thank you Jesus for walking beside me the whole way, giving me inspiration and urging me forward. My forever Friend.

About the Author

JAN LIVES WITH her husband Ed in Brownsmead, Oregon near the Columbia River. They live on a farm where Ed raises sheep, U-pick blueberries, U-cut Christmas trees and also pumpkins to give to the grade school children.

In this old farmhouse they have raised ten children and five exchange students. They sponsor twenty-one children through Unbound.org.

Jan is a retired elementary teacher and theater director. She is active in her church where she leads worship, Bible studies and speaks at retreats. In her spare time, she gardens, knits, quilts, writes and builds relationships.